What's In A Word?

by

David Zaslow

illustrated by Grace Henson

This book is dedicated to my wife, Debra

Cover design by Grace Henson

Copyright © Good Apple, Inc., 1983

ISBN No. 0-86653-148-3

Printing No. 987

GOOD APPLE, INC.
BOX 299
CARTHAGE, IL 62321-0299

TABLE OF CONTENTS

Introduction

My cousin said to her three-year-old son, "Come on, Alex; we're going." In frustration Alex replied, "I am come **oning**!" As a tourist in France my father went to a restaurant and ordered a cup of Sanka. The waiter brought him five cups of coffee, **cinque** coffee. When I was a child my mother told me that we were going to **Miami** Beach, which I promptly began calling "my mommy's **Ami** Beach." Younger children will "accidently" invent wonderful words like **lasterday, amn't,** and **outen.** To their open minds **lasterday** is as good as **yesterday,** and **amn't** is as logical as **isn't.** If you can **brighten** a room you can certainly **outen** the lights. Children have an intuitive grasp of the creative possibilities in language. While we work to "standardize" their language we should also be aware that their word-inventions are creative.

What's in a word? The warmth, humor, creativity, and fallibility of everyday people trying to say what they mean. A journey into the history of language is an adventure into the lives of people and their cultures. There are about 700,000 words in our language, though most of us only use about 20,000 of them. About 80% of our everyday words derive from Anglo-Saxon, also called Old English, which was spoken from 450-1100 A.D. Another 15% derive from Greek and Latin, and 5% from other languages. The more technical our language, the more we depend upon words that have been borrowed from Greek and Latin. Because English has borrowed words from so many languages, there are many synonyms. We have the choice of saying the same thing in different ways. Anglo-Saxon, for example, gives us the word **house.** If we want to be more formal, we can substitute **house** with the word **residence** which comes from Latin.

Every word is a one-word poem. Beneath the surface of a word's meaning is its original meaning. These two meanings of a word have a poetic impact upon us when we consider them side by side. We gain a sense of a thing in its relationship to something else. The word **daisy,** for example, derives from an Anglo-Saxon word meaning "day's eye." In our minds the metaphor of the eye of day is juxtaposed with our sense of a particular flower. If we think about the relationship between these two different images, we experience the poetry and magic that is inherent in every word. One thing is used to represent, signify, or suggest something else.

Language reflects consciousness, and in turn helps to shape consciousness. The way people experience the world can be seen in the structure of their languages. There are many languages of primitive cultures that contain no real nouns. The world is experienced as an active and vibrant series of changing states. The Wintu Indians have no definitive clause. Instead of saying "the sky is blue," a Wintu might say "the sky, it seems to be blue." Many primitive societies do not differentiate singular from plural, past from present, or the animate from the inanimate. The individual is seen as part of the many, the past as part of the present, and the inanimate as part of the animate. On the other hand, some primitive languages have very complex features. There are Eskimo languages that distinguish a dozen types of snow. One Northwest Indian language distinguishes three kinds of past, and a native Australian language has five future tenses. The Paiute Indians have many compound verbs like **sit-talk,** and there is one language spoken by people in India that does not separate adjectives from nouns. Words like **sad-day** help these people express more accurately the way they experience the world. Over 40% of the Bushman's language is onomatopoeic and is very beautiful to listen to. New experiential opportunities are opened and closed with every nuance in every language. The Chinese language, as complex as it might seem, does not differentiate gender, number, or tense. It is a timeless and flexible language made of single words that can be used as either nouns, verbs, or adjectives.

It must be said that no system of morphology, grammar, or syntax is better than another. Each offers its own advantages and disadvantages. Our "standard" English is simply what is agreed upon. At one time double negatives were permissible in "standard" English. Today they are not. Someday they may be permissible again. There is nothing inherently good or bad about the use of double negatives. The way English is used reflects the poetry and beauty of the people who speak or write it. The responsible teacher must, of course, teach "standardized" English, but must also be sensitive to the backgrounds of the children being taught. An American Indian child might write "the horse was still run" or "I saw a crane, two of them." A Black American child might write "he been go to school." A Chinese-American child might write "I see he in the night of dark." It may be a challenge to teach an older child about tense, number, and gender differentiations when in his or her native language there are no such "false" distinctions. A child from another culture will, naturally transliterate from the native language or dialect when speaking or writing in English.

If reading and writing constitute the basic skills, then language history constitutes the "basic knowlege." To learn the history of our letters can give handwriting activities deeper meaning. To learn about the changes that have taken place in spelling and word meaning can give vocabulary lessons greater sparkle. To examine the origin of words can uncover the hidden poetry which underlies all communication. These activity pages can be duplicated and handed out to your students, or simply used as starting points for your own language history lessons. Try using them in association with science and social studies lessons. Write the etymology of one word each day on a corner of your board.

On a personal note I am indebted to Jean Showalter of Harcourt Brace Jovanovich for the opportunity to do the research in language history that was used in the **Language for Daily Use** series. My sincere thanks to Jerry Aten, my editor at Good Apple, for his support and advice on the development of this book. Finally, I must express my gratitude to Mario Pei, Joseph T. Shipley, and J.N. Hook whose research and scholarship served as a foundation for this book. Whatever errors, however, are my own responsibility.

David Zaslow
Ashland, Oregon

1

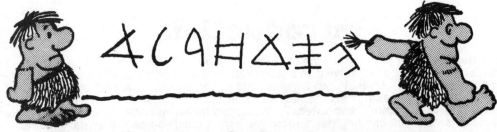

The Story of the Alphabet

Spoken language is much older than written language. The first written languages were made with pictures. They were sometimes painted or carved on rocks, and every picture stood for an object. People learned how to "read" the pictures. The ancient Egyptians invented **hieroglyphs** where pictures symbolized objects, actions, and even ideas. Some of our letters can be traced to hieroglyphics. **M** was water, **N** was a snake, **S** was a mountain. Most of the letters in our alphabet were invented by the Phoenicians. As alphabets developed the letters replaced the pictures. With our 26 letters we have created over 700,000 words. Add 27 zeros to the number 400 and you have the 400 **octillion** words that can be made with different combinations of our 26 letters. The first alphabets did not have vowels, and sometimes the words did not even have spaces between them. English is read from left to right. Hebrew is read from right to left, and Chinese is read from top to bottom.

Along with our spoken and written language, we use many **nonverbal** languages. We can "talk" using hand, face, and body **gestures** without ever saying a word. Traffic police and referees "talk" with **hand signals,** and students learn to "understand" school **bells,** fire **alarms,** and traffic **lights.** The road **signs** that we learn to "read" are modern forms of picture-writing. Deaf people can "speak" using **sign** language, and blind people can "read" with their fingers using **Braille.** The **Morse Code** uses dots and dashes to stand for letters. People have created languages with **flags, smoke, yodels, knots, notches, horns, whistles, beads,** and **drums.**

Activity

Write sentences using **only** pictures on the first two lines. On the last two lines write like the ancient Greeks: no vowels, no spaces between words, and "as the ox plows." This means writing one line left to right, and writing the next line **backwards** from right to left. It's fun!

_____

_____

_____

_____

A Short History of English

Between the years 450 and 1066 A.D. the language of **Old English,** also known as **Anglo-Saxon,** was spoken. It developed in a place called **Angle-Land,** now called **England.** African and Asian tribes probably settled in this land thousands of years ago. Around 2,000 B.C. the **Celts** conquered the **Picts.** In 55 A.D. the **Romans** then conquered the **Celts.** The Germanic tribes called **Angles, Saxons,** and **Jutes** took over this land as the Roman Empire was coming to an end in the fifth century.

These Germanic tribes created the language of **Old English.** However, they, too, were conquered by the **Scandinavians** in the ninth century. The people of **Angle-Land** began borrowing words from these **Danish Vikings,** and **Norwegians.** Most of our everyday words come from **Old English.** The Germanic tribes were farmers and gave us many simple and practical words: **love, father, mother, brother,** and **sister.** We would not be able to understand **Old English** today.

The next development in our language came in 1066 A.D. when the **Normans** from France conquered England once again. Suddenly words from Latin began pouring into Old English. Even though the Romans had conquered England before, it was not until the **Norman Invasion** that Latin words were borrowed. This influence created a newer language called **Middle English.** The language we speak today is known as **Modern English,** as more words from **Dutch, Spanish,** and **Greek** began entering our language. Will people speak some kind of **Ultra-Modern English** someday? They probably will, because "living" languages change and evolve to meet people's needs.

Activity

Guess what modern words the following **Old English** words have become:

beorhtnes _____   fot _____   heorte_____

hoefon _____   leoht_____   monan _____

niht _____   steorra _____   sunnan _____

A Spellbinding Story

Before printing was invented there were no standard rules for spelling. The word **sparrow** was spelled many different ways: **sparou, sparu, sparoo, sparuwe, sperow,** and **speruwa.** After the American Revolution a man named Noah Webster had some creative ideas about spelling. He believed that words should be spelled the way they sound. He suggested dropping unnecessary silent letters that many words contain: **axe** became **ax, centre** became **center, colour** became **color, draught** became **draft, defence** became **defense, musick** became **music, plough** became **plow, programme** became **program,** and **waggon** became **wagon.**

It is not easy to change the spelling of words because so many people have to agree to the changes. Noah Webster wanted the silent **b** to be dropped from the words like **debt, doubt,** and **subtle,** but he failed to get these, and many other, logical changes accepted. Spelling changes very slowly. Today the word **catalogue** is often spelled **catalog; hiccough** is frequently spelled **hiccup; doughnut** is sometimes spelled **donut;** and **through** is occasionally spelled **thru.** The spelling of words will probably be simplified even more in the future. Those lucky kids!

Activity

Here are some of the simplified spellings that have been suggested and rejected in the last two centuries. Some of them might be accepted in the future. Write the "correct" spelling next to each word. On the bottom two lines write other words that you would like to see simplified.

alfabet _____ buz _____ eg _____

emfasis _____ fonograf _____ gard _____

hav _____ iland _____ rime _____

nite _____ tho _____ wisht _____

_____ _____ _____

_____ _____ _____

Do You Speak British or American?

The English language is spoken in America, Great Britain, and in some of the countries that were once colonies of the British Empire. There are slight differences in the way people speak in America and in England. Accents are different, and even some words and spellings are different. In England an **automobile** is a **motor car,** and a **truck** is a **lorrey. A trunk** is called a **boot,** and a **muffler** is a **silencer. A hood** is a **bonnet,** and a **bumper** is a **buffer.** When you want some **gas** just ask for **petrol,** and while you're there please ask the chap to clean the **windscreen.**

The word **jail** is sometimes spelled **gaol** in England, and the word **theater** is spelled **theatre.** Following is a list of words with their British spellings. Write the American spellings in the blank spaces. You can use a **dictionary.**

axe _____   centre _____

cheque _____   civilise _____

colour _____   connexion _____

cyder _____   flavour _____

grey _____   honour _____

jewellery _____   labour _____

odour _____   neighbour _____

offence _____   programme _____

pyjamas _____   storey _____

traveller _____   waggon _____

5

An American-British Dictionary
A to N

An American student makes a **period** at the end of a sentence. A British student makes a **full stop.** Following is a list of American words along with their British counterparts. Just for fun try writing a few sentences using British words instead of American words.

apartment = flat
bathrobe = dressing gown
bobby pin = hair grip
closet = cupboard
cookie = sweet biscuit
diapers = nappies
drizzle = light fog
freight train = goods train
fried eggs = fries
get in line = queue up
kindergarten = infant's school
landslide = landslip
mail a letter = post a letter
movie = cinema

baby carriage = pram
biscuits = scones
candy store = sweet shop
clothing store = haberdashers
cracker = biscuit
druggist = chemist
elevator = lift
french fries = chips
garbage can = dustbin
hardware store = ironmonger
lawyer = solicitor
long distance call = trunk call
merry-go-round = roundabout
napkin = serviette

An American-British Dictionary
N to Z

newsstand = kiosk
pantry = larder
potato chips = crisps
railroad tracks = railway
  metals
shoelaces = **bootlaces**
sneakers = plimsoles
spool = reel
stroller = pushcar
TV = telly
toilet = water closet
trolly = tram
undershirt = vest
vest = waistcoat
vegetable store = greengrocer

oatmeal = porridge
pants = trousers
railroad = railway
rare = underdone
shopping bag = carrier
soft drink = minerals
suspenders = braces
subway = underground
ticket agent = booking clerk
trash = rubbish
umbrella = brolly
vacation = holiday
weatherman = clerk of the
  weather
z = zed

What American students call **quotation marks** the British students call **inverted commas.** Write a short dialogue between an American student and a British student, each of them using their own words.

_____

_____

_____

_____

_____

7

Obsolete Words

There are many older words in English that are no longer used. The Old English word **mood** was spelled **mod.** It was joined to other words to describe feelings. A **glaed-mod** was a "glad mood" or "kindness." A **mod-ge-thanc** was a "mood of thanks." A **mod-gemynd** was a "mood of mind" or "thoroughness." A **mod-lufu** was a "mood of love." A **mod-craeft** was a "mood of craft" or "intelligence." A **mod-full** was a "full mood" meaning "arrogance." Here are some of the more poetic **obsolete** words.

afterthink: joins the words **after** and **think** and means "repeat." If we **think** about bad things **after** we do them, we may "repent."

dearworth: joins the words **dear** and **worth** and means "beloved." Someone who is "beloved" is both **dear** to us, and **worth** a lot.

earsport: joins the words **ear** and **sport** and means "music." Figuratively, "music is a kind of **sport** for our **ears.**

eyebite: joins the words **eye** and **bite** and means "fascinate." Figuratively, our eyes **bite** things when we are "fascinated."

foresayer: joins the words **fore** and **say** and means "prophet." If we **say** something **before** it happens we are being "prophetic."

Activity

The word **wan** means "bad" or "without." It was used in several words that are now obsolete. The word **wan-luck** means "bad luck" or "misfortune." Draw lines between the obsolete words on the left and the modern words that have replaced them on the right.

wan-trust	**folly**
wan-wit	**wicked**
wan-thrift	**despair**
wan-grace	**suspicion**
wan-hope	**extravagance**

What's Your Ekename?

THEY CALL ME LONGFELLOW.

Many **family** names, or **last** names began as **nicknames.** The word **nickname** comes from the language of Anglo-Saxon, also known as Old English. It was called an **ekename** which means "added name." Many famous people had **ekenames** for last names like **Catherine the Great,** and **Richard the Lion-hearted.** Today **nicknames** are used instead of first names. Have you heard of **Stonewall Jackson**? An ancient Egyptian tomb has the name of a person named **Senni** on it. It was discovered later that **Senni** was a nickname meaning "shorty."

Last names that began as **nicknames** describe things about the people they were given to: **Armstrong, Brown, Longfellow, Noble,** and **White.** Some names have to be translated from other languages: **Boyd** means "yellow-haired." **Cameron** means "twisted nose." **Schwartz** means "dark." **Wang** means "prince." **Blum** means "flower." Many of the original native American Indian names are descriptive and poetic like **Hungry Wolf** and **Sitting Bull.**

Nicknames that become last names sometimes have interesting, even humorous, connections to other names: **Black** and **White, Branch** and **Root, Flower** and **Weed, Hand** and **Foote, High** and **Lowe, Hill** and **Dale, Locke** and **Key, Moon** and **Star, Rich** and **Poor, Salt** and **Pepper, Short** and **Long, Shy** and **Bold, Wolfe** and **Lamb.**

Activity

Look in a telephone book for other interesting last names. On the lines below invent two last **ekenames** for yourself. One should describe something good about you, and the other should be humorous. For example, **Sammy Great-writer,** and **Sammy Lazybones.**

I LIKE YOUR KNEES!

_____

_____

_____

What's in a First Name?

Every name has a poetic meaning. The name Mark, for example, means "bright." The name Brenda means "flaming sword." At one time people could hear the meaning of a name when they spoke it. While saying "Hello, Brenda," they would be thinking, "Hello, Flaming Sword." Have you ever heard the names of great native American leaders like **Sitting Bull** or **Crazy Bear**? Find out the poetic meaning of your own name.

Aaron: he who is exalted
Arnold: eagle of strength
Bernard: bold bear
David: beloved
Edward: guard of goods
Eliot: hunter
Frank: free
Gabriel: strength of God
Harvey: noble warrior
Isaac: laughter
John: the Lord is gracious
Joseph: he shall increase
Keith: windy
Leo: lion
Noah: rest
Peter: rock
Samuel: heard of the Lord
Theodore: gift of God
Victor: conqueror

Amy: beloved
Audrey: noble helper
Bonnie: little good one
Debra: bee
Cynthia: goddess of the moon
Daisy: eye of the day
Esther: star
Eve: life
Gloria: fame
Helen: dawn-bright
Jennifer: white wave
Joyce: merry
Karen: pure
Laura: the tree
Nicole: conqueror
Pamela: sweet one
Rachel: lamb of God
Valarie: healthy
Wendy: wanderer

Activity

Find out the meaning of your first name from a dictionary, name book, or from your parents. Find out the meaning of your middle name if you have one. Write the meaning of your name on the line below.

Your first name _____

Meaning _____

10

What's in a Last Name?

Until the fourteenth century most Europeans only had first names. As last names came into use, they described **careers, places, parents,** and the **people** themselves. Your name might have been **Nancy the Potter, Milty from Minnesota, Rachel, Daughter of David,** or **Debra the Beautiful.** Here are just a few last names from careers: **Baker, Bauer** (farmer), **Carpenter, Day** (dairyman), **Foster** (forester), **Fletcher** (arrow-maker), **Hunter, Wagner** (wagon-maker), **Webster,** and **Zimmerman** (carpenter in German).

Some last names are from cities and countries: **English, French, El Greco, Israel, London, Scott, Welch,** and **York.** There are local place names, too: **Bridges, Field, Ford,** and **Glenn.** Other names have to be translated. **Bach** is "brook" in German. **Steinberg** is "stone mountain" in Yiddish. **Vanderburg** is "of the city" in Dutch, and **Yamamoto** is "foot of the mountain" in Japanese.

Another kind of last name is made by adding the first name of a parent to the child's first name. A Hebrew name might be **David, Son of Samuel.** Modern names contain shorter forms of the words "son of" or "daughter of." Last names may begin with **Ben, De, Mac, Mc, Ni, O,** or **Up.** For example: **Ben Gurion, De Pierre, MacDonald, McCoy, Ni Hogan, O'Brian,** or **Upjohn.** Last names may end with the letters **ez, ich, ova, sen, son, sohn, ski,** or **s.** For example: **Alvarez, Ivanovich, Ivanova, Hensen, Johnson, Mendelssohn, Petroski,** or **Williams.**

Activity

Write the national origin and meaning of your last name on line one. On line two rename yourself for something you like doing: **Kim the Jogger.** On line three use the words "son of" or "daughter of" between your first name and the first name of a parent: **Nathan, Son of Jeff.**

1. _____

2. _____

3. _____

GUESS WHY MY NAME IS FLETCHER?

MY LAST NAME IS POTTER.

IS YOUR LAST NAME CARPENTER?

Words from the Native Americans

When the first European settlers came to America they were warmly greeted by the native people who had already lived here for thousands of years. The Europeans probably would not have survived without help from the native American Indians who introduced them to foods and animals they had never even heard of. Many practical Indian words became part of English: **raugraouchcun** became **raccoon, segankw** became **skunk, moosu** became **moose,** otchuck became **woodchuck,** jonakin became **johnnycake,** and **squanterquashe** was shortened to **squash.** The settlers watched the native American people play a game called **chunkey** and were inspired to invent **hockey.** The Iroquois Nation had a democratic constitution which helped inspire the writing of the United States Constitution. George Washington even used Indian fighting methods to help win the Revolution.

The names of thousands of rivers, streams, lakes, streets, towns, cities, and counties come from the many native American languages. Twenty-six state names come from Indian languages. Guess the state names that come from the following native American words:

Word	Meaning	State
al·ay·es·ka	great country	_____
alibamu	I clear the thicket	_____
quonecktacut	river of pines	_____
eda·hoe	light on the mountain	_____
maesi·sipu	fish river	_____
mich·gama	great water	_____
ouiscousin	meeting of the rivers	_____
tejas	allies	_____

Talking Leaves

As leaves are shaken by the wind it almost seems as if they have voices. Can you imagine words on a page as leaves on a tree? Our eyes are like winds blowing through each of the letters. These are the poetic thoughts that a brilliant Cherokee Indian named Sequoyah might have had. Sequoyah was born in 1770 in the Cherokee territory of Tennessee. As a man he was amazed by the messages that white people could send to each other on pieces of paper. Words that looked like leaves could be read and understood. He called them "talking leaves."

Sequoyah was partially crippled from a hunting accident, and he spent his time working to invent a system of writing for his own Cherokee language. His relatives called him a dreamer. His friends thought he was a little crazy. People called him a child, but Sequoyah had a dream. People made fun of him, but his dream was a great idea. He spent many hours alone in the woods making designs in the earth out of sticks and stones. At first, he tried to create a symbol for every Cherokee word. But there were too many words. In 1810, after twelve years of work, Sequoyah invented a **syllabary** made of 86 symbols. Unlike an alphabet the symbols in a **syllabary** represent the syllables in a language. Sequoyah's system was so simple that it took only a few days to learn. In an incredibly short time almost all of the Cherokee people could read and write. Sequoyah had earned the respect of his people. To this day no one person in the whole world has ever done what Sequoyah did.

He started the first American Indian newspaper, helped write a constitution for his people, and translated the Bible. Most of all he gave the Cherokees the power of the "talking leaves." It was tragic that the white people forced Sequoyah and his people from their ancient homeland. They marched on the "trail of tears" where thousands of native Americans died. Sequoyah was a dreamer, and he worked to make his dream real. He will not be forgotten.

Activity

Use your dictionary to find out what great tree was named for Sequoyah. Write your answer below.

The Poetry of Words

Fossils are found in rocks, but they are also found in words. They are the poetic pictures inside the history of all words and are called **fossil-metaphors.**

anenome: imagine this beautiful flower as the "daughter of the wind." This is exactly what this fragrant sounding word meant in Greek.

anthology: imagine a book of poems or stories written by several people as a "gathering of flowers." This is what the word **anthology** actually meant in Greek. In the imagination books do contain "flowers."

astronaut: invented by combining the words "star" and "sailor." In a way the people who travel in space are "star sailors." Imagine outer space as a vast wavy sea that our ships can sail upon.

brood: when chickens **brood** they sit on eggs. When we **brood** over something, we are worrying about something. From an Old English word meaning "sitting on eggs." When people **brood** they "sit on the eggs of thoughts and feelings." Have you "hatched" any good ideas lately?

crater: imagine the **crater** of a volcano as a huge "cup." The earth could be its saucer. From the Greek word **krater** meaning "cup."

calculate: how would you like to "pebble" the answer? Counting was once done with stones, and the Latin word **calculus** meant "pebble."

Activity

The French word **carriere** first meant "road." From it the word **career** evolved which describes people's jobs. Write a short nonrhyming poem describing how a **career** or a particular job is like a **road.**

_____

_____

_____

_____

The Poetry of Words

atom: one of the smallest particles. From a Greek word meaning "not to cut" since it was so small. The Latin word **atomus** means "the twinkling of an eye" which was considered the smallest measure of time.

cloak: a loose fitting robe-coat. From the Late Latin word **clocca** meaning "bell" since **cloaks** look like bells. The word **clock** has the same origin since the first clocks were really bells.

coconut: from the Portuguese word **coco** meaning "funny-ugly-smiling-face," and the Latin word **concha** meaning "skull." A coconut is a "funny-ugly-smiling-face-skull-nut." The slang word **conk** comes from **concha**. When **coconuts** fall from trees they can **conk** you on the head.

concrete: The Latin word **crescere** means "to grow." It has given us the word **creature.** Add the Latin word **con** meaning "together" to it, and we have **concrete**, something that seems to "grow together."

daisy: from the Old English word **daeges-eage** meaning "day's eye." A very beautiful metaphor describing the way this flower looks.

dandelion: from Latin through the French words **dent de lion** meaning "tooth of a lion." Do the petals look like lion's teeth to you?

Activity

An **easel** is a stand used for displaying things. It is from the Dutch word **ezel** meaning "donkey." Name **nonliving** things that can be compared to the following animals. For example, "The **star** is like a **firefly**."

The _____ is like a **hippo**.

The _____ is like an **octopus**.

The _____ is like a **butterfly**.

The _____ is like a **cobra**.

The Poetry of Words

expect: from the Latin words **ex** + **spectare** meaning "looking out." Here we have the origin making the meaning of the word more concrete.

fathom: a six-foot measurement of the depth of water. From Old English meaning "outstretched arms." Body parts were used to measure many things.

fret: when you worry about something does it "eat away" at you? The word **fret** actually comes from an Old English word meaning "eat away."

gladiola: from Latin. The Roman **gladiator** was a "swordsman," but this flower's name simply means "little sword" which describes its looks.

govern: from the Latin word meaning "to steer." Many popular comparisons have been made between **governing** and "steering" the "ship of state."

intellect: from the Latin **inter** + **legere** meaning "to choose between." The origin gives us a concrete picture of the meaning of the word **intellect**.

minute: from the Latin word **minutus** meaning "small." A **minute** is not something we can see, but knowing that it is "small" makes a picture in our minds.

Activity

The word **muscle** comes from the Latin word meaning "mouse." The Romans had great imaginations. Write a nonrhyming poem that compares body parts to animals. For example, "My finger is like a worm."

My _____ is like a _____ .

My _____ is like a _____ .

My _____ is like a _____ .

My _____ is like a _____ .

The Poetry of Words

answer: in court we "swear" our **answers** are true. **Answer** comes from the Old English word **andswerian** meaning "to swear against." The root comes from a Greek word meaning "sound" which has also given us the word **swarm**. Teachers never **swear** when **swarmed** with **answers**.

pedigree: from the French words **pie de grue** meaning "a crane's foot." Records of ancestors and lines of family descent were made with forked lines that resembled the foot of a crane.

perceive: from the Latin word meaning "to grasp" or "to catch." We figuratively "catch on to" or "grasp hold of" ideas when we **perceive** them.

penicillin: from the Latin word **penicillus** meaning "pencil" or "brush." Feathers were used as the first **pencils,** and **penicillin** was first made from a fungus that looks like a feather or a brush when it grows.

perplexed: from the Latin words **per** + **plectere** meaning "thoroughly woven." When we are **perplexed** our thoughts are figuratively "woven" in a way that is confusing. Never "spin a yarn" that is too **perplexing**.

ponder: from the Latin word **ponderare** meaning "to weigh." It helps us to understand a mental activity by picturing it as something concrete.

Activity

A **pommel** is the knob on a saddle, or the ball at the end of a sword. The word is from the French word meaning "apple" because of its shape. Name living things that look like very different nonliving things.

A _____ looks like a _____ .

A _____ looks like a _____ .

A _____ looks like a _____ .

A _____ looks like a _____ .

The Poetry of Words

There are pictures hidden in the history of every word. Poetry makes pictures out of words, and every word has a poem inside of it.

reflect: a mirror "bends back" light to create a **reflection.** When our mind **reflects** on something, we are figuratively "bending back" our thoughts. From the Latin word **reflectere** meaning "bend back."

result: from the Latin word **resilire** meaning "to leap back." A **result** is figuratively a "leap back" from an action to a solution. Maybe we "leap back" in surprise when we receive our math test **results.**

salary: from the same Latin word **salt.** When you work hard you figuratively "earn your salt." The Romans used the word **salarium** figuratively to mean "money to buy salt." Today we receive **salaries** unless we're "not worth our salt."

seminar: teachers attend **seminars** where they gather the "seeds of knowledge." From the Latin word **seminarium** meaning "seed-garden." A **seminary** was once a real garden. Now it is a place to learn. When teachers **disseminate** ideas they are "scattering seeds."

Activity

Your library has a **thesaurus** which is a dictionary of synonyms. The word comes from Greek and means "treasure." Write a short nonrhyming poem describing the connection between a book and a treasure. How is a book like, or not like, a real treasure?

_____

_____

_____

_____

The Poetry of Words

investigate: from the Latin word **in + vestigium** meaning "into footprint." Sherlock Holmes gets "into footprints" during **investigations.**

test: from the Latin word **testa,** the earthen pots once used for trying metals. Today a spelling **test** can figuratively "cook you in a pot."

text: from the Latin **textum** meaning "to weave." Today a **text** is a book, or the words in a book. Figuratively, a **text** "weaves" words.

time: time and **tide** once had identical meanings in English. Ocean tides measure time. **Yuletide** is not a tide, but the "time" of Christmas.

trivial: small and unimportant matters. From the Latin **tres + viae** meaning "three roads." People used to have unimportant "small talk" at crossroads, places where roads meet each other.

Activity

The word **window** comes from an older English word **wind-oge** meaning "wind-eye." Name things that can be figuratively described as parts of the body? In the first space name an **object.** In the second space name a **body part.** In the third space name something from nature. For example, "The **window** is the **eye** of the **wind.**"

The _____ is the _____ of the _____.

The _____ is the _____ of the _____.

The _____ is the _____ of the _____.

The _____ is the _____ of the _____.

Words from Latin

About fifteen percent of our everyday English words come from the ancient languages of Latin and Greek. Most of the Latin words have entered our language through French.

adore: from the word **adorare** meaning "to pray to." When you adore something you show it love. Prayer expresses our love for God.

animal: from the word **anima** meaning "breath of life." A cartoonist gives the "breath of life" to his or her drawings. Another word for cartoonist is **animator.**

bus: from the word **omnibus** meaning "for all." A bus holds many people and in a way it does seem to be "for all."

cabbage: from the word **caput** meaning "head." It received its name from the way it looks. When you go to the store and buy a head of cabbage, you are really buying a head of "head."

circus: from a word which is spelled the same way meaning "circle." A three-ring circus has three circles for the different acts.

detergent: from the word **detergere** meaning "to wipe away." Since a detergent is used to clean things it helps you "wipe away" dirt.

Activity
The word **umbrella** comes from the word **umbra** meaning "shade." Guess at the connection between the original meaning and the meaning of the modern word.

_____

_____

The letters of our alphabet come from Latin, although the word **alphabet** comes from Greek. Latin was spoken by the Romans. Many useful words have come from Latin: **abracadabra, art, money, noun,** and **verb.**

envy: from the word **invidia** meaning "to see into." Envy is the feeling that you want something someone else has. In a way you have to "see into" them to know what you want.

fan: from the word **fanaticus** meaning "one who worships." In a way a modern sports fan does "worship" a team or a player.

fence: from the word **defendere** meaning "to keep away." A fence may no longer help defend your home, but it does "keep away" the dogs.

fool: from the word **follis** meaning "a pair of windbags." Lungs are like windbags, and we all need our lungs to talk foolishly.

fruit: from the word **frui** meaning "to enjoy." Fruit is sweet, and sweetness gives enjoyment. So eat your apple and "enjoy" it.

humor: from the word **humere** meaning "to be moist." Body fluids were once called **humors** and were described as giving us feelings: happy, angry, and sad. Today humor is associated with a good feeling only.

Activity
The word **isolation** comes from the word **insula** meaning "island." Guess at the connection between the original meaning of the word and the meaning of the modern word.

_____

_____

Words from Latin

manuscript: from the words **manus** meaning "hand" and **scribere** meaning "writing." If you write in **script** you are "writing by hand." Do you have good **handwriting**? Writers submit **manuscripts** to publishers even though they are not "written by hand."

missile: from the word **missilis** meaning "to send" or "to throw." A rock can be a missile if it is "thrown." Most of us think of missiles as the rockets that we "send" into space.

onion: from the word **unio** meaning "unity." The layers of an onion are all "unified." When people **unite** they are like layers in an onion.

power: from the word **potentis** meaning "I am able." The power company must "be able" to supply electricity. Boxers use their **power** when they go **pow-pow-pow,** because they are "able-able-able."

universe: from the words **unum** meaning "one" and **versum** meaning "turn." We turn on the earth, and the earth turns in the solar system. The solar system turns in the galaxy, and the galaxy turns in the universe. The universe is all that turns, but the universe only gets "one turn."

vegetable: from the word **vegetare** meaning "to enliven." Vegetables are alive, and they "enliven" the earth and your lunch.

Activity
The Latin word **spirare** means "to breathe." Many English words have come from this one root word: **aspire, expire, inspire, respire, spirit,** and **spiritual.** What is the meaning of the word **spirit** in these lines?

School **spirit** _____   A **spirited** debate _____

Supernatural **spirit** _____   The **spirit** of fun _____

22

SIT DRACO!
BE QUIETO!

Words from Latin

Fact: Thirty percent of our literacy and scientific words come from Latin.

Activity: Each of the following sentences contains one Latin word which is in bold. Can you guess what each word means in English? You can guess at the meanings from their context in the sentences. Write your answers in the blank spaces.

1. The ship had an **ancora** to hold it in place. _____
2. They built an **arca** to sail on the ocean. _____
3. The classroom has a **buxus** full of crayons. _____
4. The teacher writes with **calcem** on the board. _____
5. Everyone sat in a large **circulus.** _____
6. The children saw a **cometa** in the sky. _____
7. After dinner I wash my own **disc.** _____
8. I read about a monster called a **draco.** _____
9. Today I learned a **facto** about Latin. _____
10. Once I was sick with a very high **febris.** _____
11. I went to a **hospitalium** when I was ill. _____
12. Life is a great **miraculum.** _____
13. I like to study and explore **natura.** _____
14. The **publicus** is invited to school tonight. _____
15. We must be very **quieto** in the library. _____
16. I have learned how to **scribere** in cursive. _____

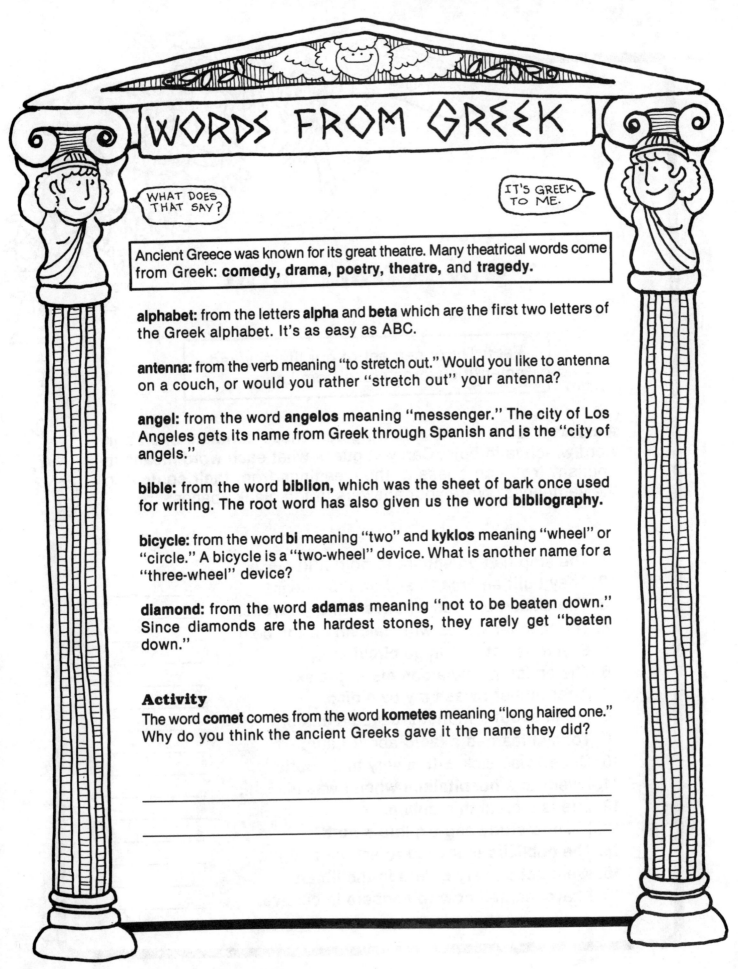

WORDS FROM GREEK

WHAT DOES THAT SAY?

IT'S GREEK TO ME.

Ancient Greece was known for its great theatre. Many theatrical words come from Greek: **comedy, drama, poetry, theatre,** and **tragedy.**

alphabet: from the letters **alpha** and **beta** which are the first two letters of the Greek alphabet. It's as easy as ABC.

antenna: from the verb meaning "to stretch out." Would you like to antenna on a couch, or would you rather "stretch out" your antenna?

angel: from the word **angelos** meaning "messenger." The city of Los Angeles gets its name from Greek through Spanish and is the "city of angels."

bible: from the word **biblion,** which was the sheet of bark once used for writing. The root word has also given us the word **bibliography.**

bicycle: from the word **bi** meaning "two" and **kyklos** meaning "wheel" or "circle." A bicycle is a "two-wheel" device. What is another name for a "three-wheel" device?

diamond: from the word **adamas** meaning "not to be beaten down." Since diamonds are the hardest stones, they rarely get "beaten down."

Activity
The word **comet** comes from the word **kometes** meaning "long haired one." Why do you think the ancient Greeks gave it the name they did?

_____

_____

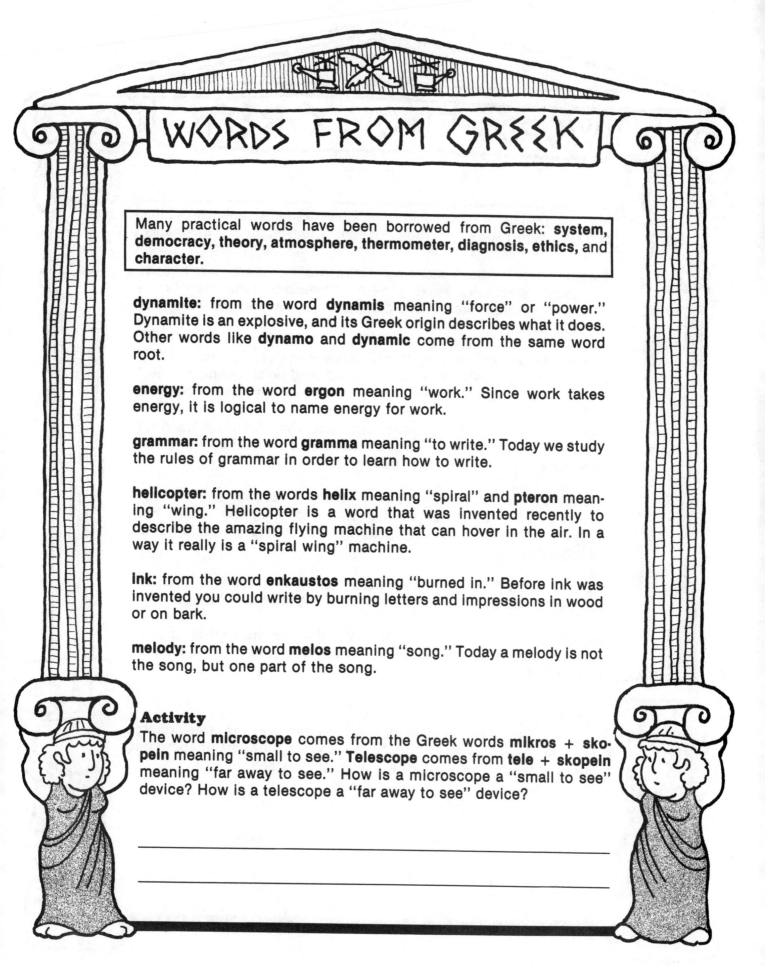

WORDS FROM GREEK

Many practical words have been borrowed from Greek: **system, democracy, theory, atmosphere, thermometer, diagnosis, ethics,** and **character.**

dynamite: from the word **dynamis** meaning "force" or "power." Dynamite is an explosive, and its Greek origin describes what it does. Other words like **dynamo** and **dynamic** come from the same word root.

energy: from the word **ergon** meaning "work." Since work takes energy, it is logical to name energy for work.

grammar: from the word **gramma** meaning "to write." Today we study the rules of grammar in order to learn how to write.

helicopter: from the words **helix** meaning "spiral" and **pteron** meaning "wing." Helicopter is a word that was invented recently to describe the amazing flying machine that can hover in the air. In a way it really is a "spiral wing" machine.

ink: from the word **enkaustos** meaning "burned in." Before ink was invented you could write by burning letters and impressions in wood or on bark.

melody: from the word **melos** meaning "song." Today a melody is not the song, but one part of the song.

Activity

The word **microscope** comes from the Greek words **mikros + skopein** meaning "small to see." **Telescope** comes from **tele + skopein** meaning "far away to see." How is a microscope a "small to see" device? How is a telescope a "far away to see" device?

_____

_____

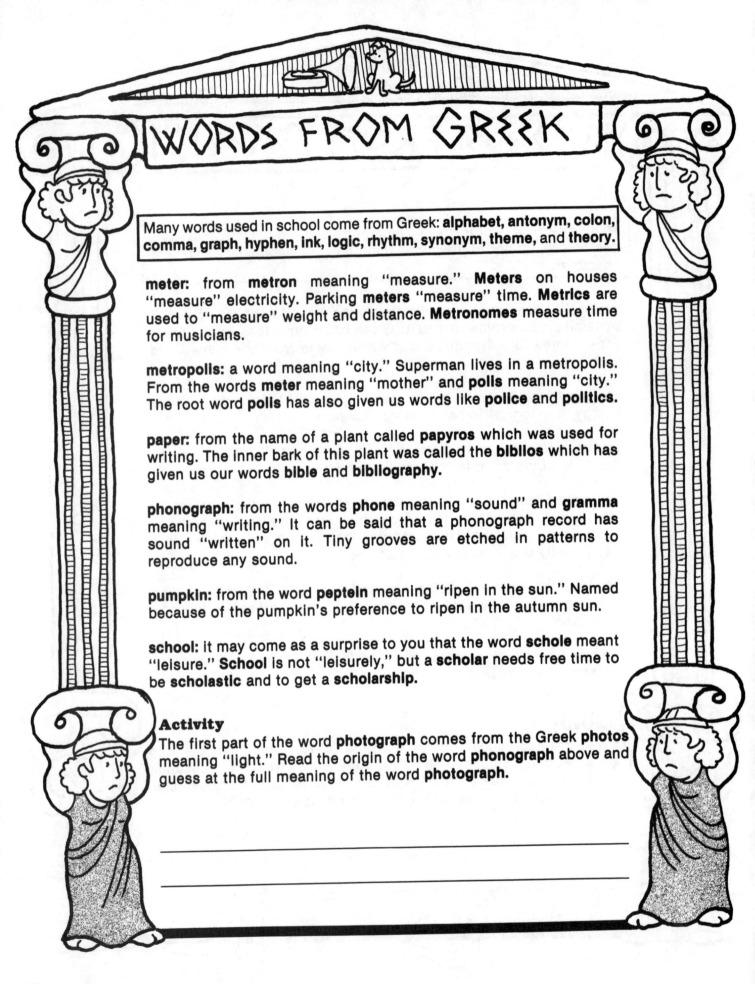

WORDS FROM GREEK

Many words used in school come from Greek: **alphabet, antonym, colon, comma, graph, hyphen, ink, logic, rhythm, synonym, theme,** and **theory.**

meter: from **metron** meaning "measure." **Meters** on houses "measure" electricity. Parking **meters** "measure" time. **Metrics** are used to "measure" weight and distance. **Metronomes** measure time for musicians.

metropolis: a word meaning "city." Superman lives in a metropolis. From the words **meter** meaning "mother" and **polis** meaning "city." The root word **polis** has also given us words like **police** and **politics.**

paper: from the name of a plant called **papyros** which was used for writing. The inner bark of this plant was called the **biblios** which has given us our words **bible** and **bibliography.**

phonograph: from the words **phone** meaning "sound" and **gramma** meaning "writing." It can be said that a phonograph record has sound "written" on it. Tiny grooves are etched in patterns to reproduce any sound.

pumpkin: from the word **peptein** meaning "ripen in the sun." Named because of the pumpkin's preference to ripen in the autumn sun.

school: it may come as a surprise to you that the word **schole** meant "leisure." **School** is not "leisurely," but a **scholar** needs free time to be **scholastic** and to get a **scholarship.**

Activity
The first part of the word **photograph** comes from the Greek **photos** meaning "light." Read the origin of the word **phonograph** above and guess at the full meaning of the word **photograph.**

_____

_____

An Electrifying Etymology

The word **electric** has a fascinating history. The story began millions of years ago when the gooey, sticky sap that oozed from trees was hardened on the earth's surface. As time passed, these balls of sap went through a **metamorphosis**, a complete change of form, and they turned into stones.

Next, these stones were swept up by the oceans where they were whirled, churned, and polished. Some of them landed on the shores where they were collected by the people of ancient Greece. The Greek word for "beaming sun" was **elektor**. Since the stones were yellowish and clear, the people decided to use **elektor** as the basis for naming them. They were named **electrons** which means "solid sunshine," since they resembled the sun.

The Greeks used their **electrons** for jewelry, and some of them even had insects perfectly preserved inside of them. Today we call these same stones **amber**. When **amber** stones are rubbed **static electricity** is created, the same kind of electricity that caused lightning. Centuries later, and in a different country, experiments were being done with electricity. William Gilbert, an English scientist made up the word **electricity** in the fifteenth century. He took the name from the magical Greek stones of "solid sunshine." Today there are dozens of words that have come into our language from the ancient Greek word **elektor**.

Activity

The ancient Greeks were very creative and poetic when they named their stones "solid sunshine." Would you call **glass** "solid wind"? Rename the gems and minerals listed below. Use your imagination.

diamond _____   turquoise _____

gold _____   silver _____

IT MUST RUN ON BATTERIES!

The Incredible Chinese Language

The Chinese language does not have an alphabet. Instead it has **characters** which stand for whole words. Chinese characters are pictures, and you actually "see" the meaning of a word. Many of the letters in the English alphabet were once pictures, too. Unfortunately, they changed so much that we cannot recognize the pictures today. The letter **A** was a picture of an ox, and **B** was a house. The letter **O** was an eye, and **R** was a head. Instead of 26 letters, Chinese school children must learn 214 primary characters and 424 one-syllable characters. These characters can be combined to make over 40,000 other characters.

Chinese is a language of individual words. There are not really any parts of speech, and a noun can be used as an adjective or a verb. A verb can be used as a noun or an adjective. Just like the English words **sheep** and **deer**, there are no singular or plural words in Chinese. There are also no past, present, or future tenses. The meanings of words come from the way they are placed in sentences. Chinese words are made by combining characters. The characters of a **hand** over the **eyes** means "gazing into the distance." The characters of a **finger** in front of a **mouth** means "in the middle." The characters of a **man** looking at the **sky** means "heaven" or "day." In English two complete words can be **joined** together to make one new word as in **skyscraper** or **hairbrush.** Chinese has many of these joined words, and some of them are very poetic. The word **telegram** is made by joining the character for **lightning** with the character for **message.** It is poetic to think of a **telegram** as a "lightning message." Joining **danger** with **opportunity** makes "crisis." Joining **milk** with **skin** makes "cream." Joining **bird** with **mouth** makes "song."

Activity
Guess which word combination below makes each of these words in Chinese: **words, railroad, good, think, forest,** and **dawn.**

Sun and moon = bright

林 Tree + Tree = _____

火車 Fire + Cart = _____

旦 Sun + Horizon = _____

思 Brain + Heart = _____

言 Stream + Mouth = _____

好 Woman + Child = _____

The Story of the Zodiac

Six thousand years ago the Babylonians and Accadians began naming and studying the stars. If you look into the sky at night, you can see a milky white "belt" that seems to stretch across the sky. The Accadians called this the **Furrow of Heaven**. They imagined a great bull ploughing a field in the sky. The **Furrow of Heaven** is probably known to you as the **Milky Way**. A Greek philosopher named Aristotle described the way the stars seem to move through the **Milky Way**. He named constellations, or groups of stars, which resemble different animals. He called them the **Kyklos Zodion**. **Kyklos** means "wheel," or "circle" in Greek and has given us words like **cycle** and **bicycle**. **Zodion** means "little animal" and has given us words like **zoo** and **zoology**. Today we call these imaginary animals and characters in the sky the **Zodiac**. The twelve constellations in it were used to name months of the year. The sky was the first calendar.

Here are the names and meanings of the months used in the old calendars. **Aquarius** is the "water carrier" beginning January 21. **Pisces** is the "fish" beginning February 21. **Aries** is the "ram" beginning March 21. **Taurus** is the "bull" beginning April 21. **Gemini** is the "twins" beginning May 21. **Cancer** is the "crab" beginning June 21. **Leo** is the "lion" beginning July 21. **Virgo** is the "maiden" beginning August 21. **Libra** is the "balance scales" beginning September 21. **Scorpio** is the "scorpion" beginning October 21. **Sagittarius** is the "archer" beginning November 21. **Capricorn** is the "goat" beginning December 21.

Activity

If you look at the stars, you can see and imagine all sorts of patterns. Create a make-believe star pattern. Name it and describe what it is.

Name _____

Description _____

_____

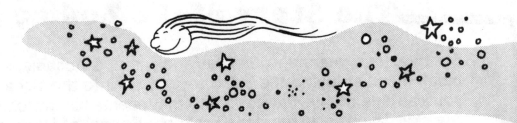

Words from Astronomy

astronomy: the science that studies planets, stars, and other celestial bodies. The word **astronomy** combines the Greek word **aster** meaning "star" and the Latin word **nomia** meaning "arrangement." The word **aster** has given us a flower and the words **asteroid, asterisk,** and **astronomical.**

comet: from the Greek **kometes** meaning "long haired one." This poetic name was given to comets because of the way they look. What we call the "tail" of a comet the Greeks thought of as "long hair." A comet's head is a **coma** from the Greek **kome** meaning "head of hair."

constellation: a group of stars is called a constellation. The Big Dipper is part of a constellation known as **Ursa Major** which means "Great Bear." The word comes from the Latin **con** + **stella** meaning "together-star-state."

corona: the glowing light around the sun, moon, or a celestial body is known as the corona. During an eclipse you can see the corona around the sun or moon. From a Latin word meaning "crown."

galaxy: a constellation is a group of stars, and a galaxy is a group of constellations. Most galaxies are made up of millions of stars and other celestial bodies. Our galaxy is called the Milky Way. The word **galaxy** comes from the Greek word **gala** which means "milk."

Activity

Write a short poem beginning with these words: "My life is a galaxy...." Answer these questions in your poem. Who are the stars in your galaxy? What do the stars in your galaxy revolve around? Where is the sky?

Words from Astronomy

light-year: light travels at the incredible speed of 186,000 miles per second. A light-year is the distance that light travels in one full year which is about six trillion miles, give or take a few feet.

nebula: a mass of glowing gas or dust in outer space, and sometimes taking the shape of a ring. From the Greek word **nephos** meaning "cloud." We speak of things as **nebulous** if they are unclear or "cloudy."

quasar: very distant objects that look like stars. They seem unusually blue and emit ultraviolet light and radio waves. The word is an acronym for "quasi-stellar radio sources."

solstice: a time marking the longest day of the year (June 21) and the shortest day of the year (December 21). From the Latin words **sol** meaning "sun" and **statum** meaning "standing still."

telescope: a device invented by the Italian astronomer Galileo in the fifteenth century. Named from the Greek words **tele + ski-pein** meaning "far away seeing." A telescope can see things that are far away.

Activity

Name two other popular devices that begin with the Greek root word **tele** meaning "far away." Guess at the reason why these devices received their names. You may get a clue from reading about the word **telescope**.

_____ _____

_____

_____ _____

Extraterrestrial Words

The Bedouin people in the Middle East named stars after living things. There are four stars that are named for camels quenching their thirst in the river of the Milky Way. Most star names come from Arabic, and most constellation names come from Hebrew through Greek. There are five stars in the constellation **Virgo** that are named for barking dogs. In the constellation **Orion** there is a red star named **Betelgeuse** which means "the giant's shoulder." People sometimes call this star **Beetle-Juice**, and say that the star's name means "beetle's blood."

The stars seem to move along the "belt" of the **Milky Way**, and we have made calendars by studying their locations as the seasons change. **Astrology** has been practiced for thousands of years. The name comes from the two Greek words **aster + logos** meaning "knowledge of the stars." People have tried to predict the future by charting the locations of stars and planets, but **astrology** is not a real science. There is real evidence that the moon influences our behavior. The word **lunatic** comes from the Latin word **luna** meaning "moon." A **lunatic** is someone who is "moonstruck." The planets and stars may also affect our behavior, but it is not yet known how. People once had great faith in the influence of stars over life. Look at the history of the words **disaster** and **consider.**

Disaster comes from two Latin words: **dis** means "away" or "negative" and **aster** means "star." People believed that if the stars were "negative" towards them a **disaster** could occur. Now **consider** the word **consider.** The word also comes from two Latin words: **con + sidus** meaning "together-star." If you are **considerate** you are "together with the stars."

Activity
The **Big Dipper** is part of a constellation named **Ursa Major** which means "Great Bear." People often use poetic names for stars and constellations. Rename the **Big Dipper** using an adjective and an animal name.

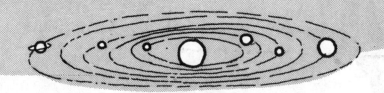

Naming the Planets

When Galileo invented the **telescope** he called it a **perspicilium**. This amazing invention had other names too: **instrumentum, occiale,** and **oranum**. A **telescope** helps us to see faraway planets and stars. The word comes from two Greek words **tele** meaning "far away" and **scopein** meaning "to look." Most of the nine known planets were named for mythological Roman gods. Since stars appear to move around in the sky, the Romans called them **stellae errantes** meaning "wandering stars."

Mercury: the Roman god of commerce. The word **mercurial** comes from the name of this god, and describes someone who has ingenuity.

Venus: the Roman goddess of love and beauty.

Mars: the Roman god of war. The word **martial** comes from his name and refers to fighting. Which month was named for him?

Jupiter: the Roman god of the sky also known as **Jove.** A phrase used to express surprise is "by Jove" which comes from his name.

Saturn: the Roman god of agriculture. The word **saturnine** means to be gloomy. What day of the week is named for this ancient god?

Uranus: named for the Greek god **Ouranous,** god of the heavens.

Neptune: the Roman god of rivers and streams.

Pluto: the Roman god of wealth, the dead, and the underworld. **Plutonium** is a radioactive element named for this god. A **plutocracy** is a government controlled by the rich.

Activity

Rename the planets using the names of your friends. You can use the endings from the names of the planets. **Mercury** could become **Maryury** for **Mary**, and **Jupiter** could become **Samiter** for **Sam.**

Mercury _____

Mars _____

Uranus _____

Earth _____

Saturn _____

Pluto _____

Venus _____

Jupiter _____

Neptune _____

33

Words from Mythology

A **myth** is a special kind of story about gods, goddesses, and all sorts of supernatural creatures and beings. Great **myths** have been created by the Egyptians, American Indians, Japanese, Chinese, Persians, Romans, Greeks, and most other ancient cultures around the world.

atlas: a book of charts or maps of the world. The word is from a Greek myth about a god named **Atlas** who was forced to hold the world and sky on his shoulders after the **Titans** were defeated by the **Olympians** in battle.

cereal: a name for different kinds of grain. The next time you eat cereal for breakfast think of **Ceres,** the Roman goddess of harvest.

chaos: a state of confusion. In Greek myths **chaos** is a substance without shape. It was said to be the original state of the universe.

clue: to solve a problem, it helps to have a **clue** or hint. In a famous Greek myth **Theseus** unwound a spool of thread behind him as he entered the labyrinth to kill a monster called the **Minotaur.** He killed the monster and followed the thread to find his way out. In Middle English a spool of thread was called a **clewe.** Today we use a clue to help us find our way out of problems.

Activity

What ocean is named for the Greek god **Atlas**? The **Olympians** were a group of Greek gods. What famous athletic event is named for them?

_____

_____

Words from Mythology

Four months, five days, and eight planets were named after gods and goddesses from Norse, Greek, and Roman myths.

geography: the science that studies the history of the earth. Named for the Greek goddess of the earth called **Gaea.** Other words from her name are **geology** and **geometry.**

gigantic: something very, very big. **Gigantis** is a Greek word used in many myths which means "the power of the gods." The word **giant** also comes from this word.

hypnosis: a method of putting people into a trance used by **hypnotists** and some doctors. Named for the Roman god of sleep called **Hypnos.**

music: in Greek myths there are nine goddesses known as **Muses.** They are the goddesses of art and science. If you are **amused** the **Muses** are "in" you. Art is shown at a **museum.** The **calliope** is an instrument named for a **Muse.** The planet **Uranus** was also named for a **Muse.**

money: named for **Juno Moneta,** the Roman goddess of warning. Her face was engraved in the first coins ever made.

Activity

Mythical beings represent things in nature. Name and describe your own mythical characters to stand for **earth, wind, water,** and **light.**

_____   _____

_____   _____

_____   _____

_____   _____

WE'RE SO AMUSING!

Words from Mythology

Mt. Olympus is a real mountain in Greece. In myths it was said to be the home of **Zeus** and the place where the gods slept.

iris: the Greek goddess of the rainbow was named **Iris.** From her name comes the name of a flower and the center of the eye.

ocean: thinking that the earth was flat, the Greeks describe a river of waters that encircled the world. They called these waters **okeanos.**

panic: the Greek god Pan, god of shepherds, lived in the forest and made scary noises at night. Today when people **panic** they are scared.

psyche: things that have to do with emotions and the mind. **Psyche** is the soul, and she became a slave to **Venus** to win back **Cupid's** love.

siren: a warning of danger. However, in Greek myths the **sirens** were creatures whose sweet songs lured ships into dangerous waters.

territory: a body of land named for **Terra,** the Roman goddess of the earth. From her name we also have the words **terrace** and **terrain.**

tantalize: something we want that we cannot have is **tantalizing. Tantalus** is the villainous son of **Jupiter** in Greek myths. He was punished for revealing some of the secrets of **Zeus** by having delicious fruits held out in front of him and then taken away whenever he tried to eat them.

volcano: this word comes from the Roman god of fire and metalworking named **Vulcan.** The word **vulcanize** also comes from his name.

Activity
Name and describe an imaginary monster who is the friendly "guardian of toys and games." What unusual things does he or she like to do?

_____

_____

_____

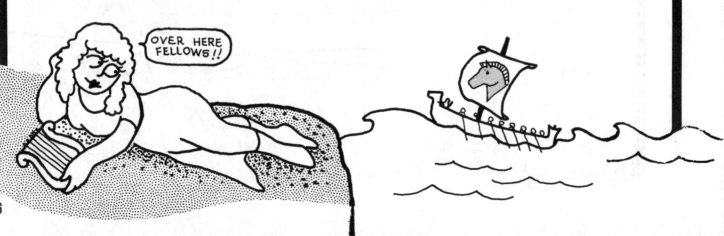

HE'S CUTE!

Naming the Days

Sunday: the word is made from the words **sun** and **day.** In Old English it was spelled **Sunnandaeg,** which was the "day of the sun."

Monday: the word is made from the words **moon** and **day.** In Old English it was spelled **Monandaeg,** which was the "day of the moon."

Tuesday: the Norse god of war was named **Tyr,** which was written in Old English as **Tiw.** He was very much like **Mars,** the Roman god of war. The Old English spelling for this day was **Tiwesdaeg.**

Wednesday: named for **Wodin,** the leader of the Norse gods, and the father of **Tiw.** He was the god of storms. In Old English this day was spelled **Wodnesdaeg.**

Thursday: named for **Thor,** the Norse god of thunder. He could hold lightning in his hands and was like the Roman god **Jupiter.** In Old English this day was spelled **Thuresdaeg.**

Friday: The Norse goddess of love was named **Friya.** She was **Wodin's** wife and the mother of **Thor.** When she was happy the sunset was full of colors. In Old English this day was spelled **Frigedaeg.**

Saturday: named for **Saturn,** the Roman god of farming and agriculture. This is the only day of the week named after a Roman god. In old English this day was spelled **Saeternesdaeg.**

Activity
Rename the day's of the week after your friends, colors, or feelings. For example, **Tuesday** could be "Bluesday" or "Amyday."

Sunday _____

Monday _____ Tuesday _____ Wednesday _____

Thursday _____ Friday _____ Saturday _____

Naming the Months

January: the Latin word **janua** means "door." January is the "door" to a new year, and **Janus** was the Roman god of doors. He had two faces. One looked to the future and one to the past. The word **janitor** shares the same origin. In Old English this month was called "Wolf-Month."

February: from the Latin word **februa** meaning "cleansing." The Romans had a ritual for purification during this month each year. In Old English this month was called "Sprouting-Cabbage-Month."

March: named for Mars, the Roman god of war, since wars often began in spring. The word **martial** and the planet **Mars** were also named for him. In Old English this month was called "Loud-Wind-Noise-Month."

April: from the Latin word **aperire** meaning "to open." In April flowers open up. The words **aperture, appear,** and **apparition** are also from the same origin. In Old English this month was called "Easter-Month."

May: from the Latin word **maior** meaning "greater." **Maia** was the mother of a god in Roman mythology. In Old English this month was called "Three-Milking-Month," a time when the cows could be milked three times.

June: this month was probably named for **Juno,** the Roman goddess and guardian of women. In Old English, June was called "Dry-Month."

Activity

Maybe you would rename January "After-Christmas-Blues-Month." Invent new names for the months listed below. They can be humorous.

January _____ February _____ March _____

April _____ May _____ June _____

NOT AGAIN!

Naming the Months

July: this name was suggested by Mark Antony, a famous Roman general, and the lover of Cleopatra. It was named to honor the great leader Julius Caesar. In Old English this month was called "Meadow-Month."

August: named for the nephew of Julius Caesar, and the first Roman emperor named **Augustus Caesar.** He wanted to have more days in his month than his uncle had in July, so he took a day from February, and made August into a 31-day month. Called "Weed-Month" in Old English.

September: from the Latin word **septem** meaning "seven." In the Roman calendar March was the first month, and September was the seventh. In Old English this month was called "Harvest-Month."

October: since September was the seventh month, then October would be the eighth month. From the Latin word **octo** meaning "eight." Called "Wine-Month" in Old English.

November: from the Latin word **novem** meaning "nine." This was the ninth month in the Roman calendar. Called "Sacrifice Month" in Old English because this was a month when cattle were sacrificed to the gods.

December: from the Latin word **decem** meaning "ten" since this was the tenth month of the year. The modern calendar was not adopted in Great Britain until the year 1752. Called "Mid-Winter-Month" in Old English.

Activity

Rename the following months of the year from animals whose actions seem to fit the months.

July _____ August _____

September _____ October _____

November _____ December _____

Words from Place Names

cantaloup: a melon named for Cantalupo, the villa in Italy where it was first grown.

china: people often call their special porcelain dishes china. It is named for the country of China where very fine porcelain was made. Today fine china is made in many countries.

chihuahua: the name of the smallest dog in the world. It was first bred by the Aztecs, who were some of the first people to live in what is now called Mexico. The dog gets its name from Chihuahua, a state in northern Mexico.

coach: trains often have coach cars, and airplanes have coach seats. The first coaches were vehicles that people travelled in, like the stagecoach. The word comes from a city in Hungary called Kocs.

dollar: a city in Germany called Joachimsthal was famous for its silver mine. Since money was made out of silver, people would exchange what they called "joachimsthalers" named after the silver mine. To make it easier to say, they called their money "thalers." This word finally changed into our word "dollar."

Activity

Name something after your town or city. You can rename something real (a food, an animal, a medicine), or create something from your imagination. Your made-up word and definition can be funny. For example, **chickenago:** chicken feather soup named for the city where it was created, Chicago.

New word _____

Description _____

_____

Words from Place Names

frankfurter: many people know this popular food by its poetic name, hot dog. Named for the West German city of Frankfurt.

hamburger: a popular food named for the West German city of Hamburg.

jeans: named for the city of Genoa in Italy where jeans were first made. Jeans are usually made of cotton or denim.

marathon: A twenty-six-mile footrace which was named for Marathon, a city in Greece. There is a story about a young man who ran all the way from Marathon to Athens announcing that the Greeks had beaten the Persians in battle. After he told his news he dropped dead.

mayonnaise: a spread used on sandwiches named for Port Mahon on an island near Spain.

palace: a kind of residence where royal and wealthy people live. Named for Palatine Hill in Italy, once famous for its beautiful homes.

spinach: a vegetable named for what is now the country of Spain.

Activity

Use your dictionary to find out the places for which the following words were named. Write your answers in the blank spaces.

artesian well _____   cologne _____

indigo _____   spaniel _____

tobacco _____   turkey _____

WE'LL CALL IT A HAMBURGER!

IS IT MADE WITH HAMSTERS?

Words from Place Names

polka: a kind of folk dance. The word comes from the Czechoslovakian word for the country of Poland.

sardine: a small fish named for Sardinia, an island of Italy.

satin: a silky fabric whose name comes from a place in China known as Tsinkiang. Tsinkiang in the Arabic language became **zaytun.** The Arabic word then came into English as **satin.**

suede: leather with a special kind of texture. The name comes from the French word for the country of Sweden.

tangerine: a fruit similar to an orange and named for the city of Tangier in Morocco.

tobacco: a plant which is grown in several states in America and named for an island of the Antilles known as Tobago.

vaudeville: a form of theatre consisting of singing, dancing, and comedy which was once very popular in the United States. The word comes from the name of a French valley, Vaux de Vire.

Activity

The following words come from the names of places. Use a dictionary to find out which places they come from. Write the answers in the blank spaces.

attic _____   lima bean _____

madras _____   muslin _____

pheasant _____   turquoise _____

AFTER MY BROTHER DEAN ??

WE'LL CALL IT A SARDINE!

42

The Naming of American Cities

1. Named after old cities in Europe: England has given us **Boston, Bristol, London, New York City,** and **Richmond.** Egypt has given us **Cairo.** Germany has given us many cities named **Berlin,** and Greece has given us **Athens, Carthage,** and **Sparta. Venice** and **Rome** come from Italy, and **Lima** comes from Peru. **Moscow** comes from Russia, and **Geneva** comes from Switzerland.

2. Named after famous people: Kit Carson gets **Carson City,** Nevada. Bill Cody gets **Cody,** Wyoming. Christopher Columbus gets **Columbus,** Ohio. Queen Elizabeth gets **Elizabeth,** New Jersey, plus several cities named **Elizabethtown.** Andrew Jackson gets many cities named **Jacksonville.** Abraham Lincoln gets **Lincoln,** Nebraska. Pocahontas gets **Pocahontas,** Arkansas.

3. Named after animals and things in nature: **Alligator, Bee, Blue Jay, Buffalo, Coal Run, Chrome, Duck, Gas City, Goosebill, Leadville, Oil City, Opal Cliffs, Pig Eye Lake,** and **Sunflower.**

4. Named for colors or geographical locations: **Blue Eye, Central Point, Hazel Green, Highland, Medford, Midway, Orange Cove, Portsmouth, Rainbow City, Redwood City, Silverhill,** and **White Sands.**

5. Named for historical events, feelings, or for a good joke: **Dismal, Drab, Echo, Harmony, Hope, Horsethief Trail, Tombstone,** and **Worry.** Let's not leave out **Dollarville,** Michigan; **Hot Coffee,** Mississippi; **Noodle,** Texas; **Social Circle,** Georgia; **Vinegar Bend,** Alabama; and **Wham,** Louisiana.

Activity

Rename the town or city that you live in or near. Use the name of someone you know, or rename it for an event that took place there, or for something funny.

I'd change _____ to _____ .

Words from People's Names

Dozens of words have been invented by using people's names. Have you heard of the **diesel** engine? It was invented by a German scientist named Rudolph Diesel in the late 1800's. The word **sandwich** was named for an Englishman whose name was Earl of Sandwich. One day he was in a hurry, and he asked for some beef between two slices of bread. A rancher from Texas named Sam Maverick liked doing things his own way. He decided not to brand his cattle, and whenever one was seen by his neighbors it was called a **maverick.** Today we think of a **maverick** as an unbranded animal, or an independent person. The word **dunce** has an interesting history. A **dunce** is defined as a dimwitted person, but a few hundred years ago the **dunces** were followers of a ridiculed scholar named Duns Scotus.

The words **watt, volt, ohm,** and **ampere** help describe things about electricity. All four of these words were named after scientists: James Watt, Alessandro Volta, Georg Simon Ohm, and Andre Marie Ampere. Russian emperors used to be called **czars.** The word comes from the name of the famous Roman leader Julius Caesar. In England a police officer is called a **bobby.** The word comes from the name of an English politician named Sir Robert Peel. The Earl of Cardigan has a sweater named after him, and when we eat melba toast we can thank Dame Nellie Melba, an Australian opera singer. It seems as though she liked eating very thin bread toasted until it was crisp.

Activity

Use your dictionary to find out who the following flowers were named for. Write the name of the person next to each of the words below.

begonia _____   camellia _____

fuchsia _____   gardenia _____

wisteria _____   zinnia _____

BOBBY?

44

Words from Names

boycott: named for Charles C. Boycott, an English landlord who was criticized for refusing to lower people's rents. Today when people boycott a product, they refuse to buy it.

braille: a method of reading and writing for blind people. Raised dots stand for letters and numbers and can be understood by touch. This method was named for Louis Braille, a French educator.

doily: a mat made of lace or linen which is used to decorate and protect furniture. Named for Mr. Doily, an English linen-draper.

Fahrenheit: named for Gabriel Fahrenheit, who invented the first mercury thermometer and a scale to measure temperature.

guillotine: a device which was used during the French Revolution to behead prisoners. It was named after Joseph Guillotin, a French doctor who advocated its use.

guppy: a small fish often kept in aquariums. Named for R.J.L. Guppy from Trinidad, who loved animals and donated many specimens to a museum in England.

Activity

Name an imaginary invention after yourself. You may use your first or last name. Write a short description of your invention.

Name of invention _____

Description _____

_____

_____

Words from Names

leotard: a kind of clothing that fits very tightly and often used by dancers and gymnasts. It was named for Jules Leotard, a French trapeze artist and aerial gymnast. Leotards are often called **tights** because of the way they fit.

lynch: at one time when a mob was angry, they might lynch someone without a fair trial. This illegal method of killing was named for Colonel William Lynch, an American soldier.

mesmerize: a German physician named Franz Mesmer developed a way to hypnotize his patients. He used hypnosis to help his patients get well. Today we say that we are mesmerized by something when we are spellbound by it.

nicotine: a chemical substance found in tobacco leaves and named for Jean Nicot, a French scientist.

pasteurize: a method for killing the germs in foods like milk. Named for Louis Pasteur, a French physician who helped show the world that germs can cause illness.

pickle: a cucumber, or any kind of food, that has been soaked in a brine or vinegar solution. Named for William Beukelz, who pickled fish in Holland about five hundred years ago.

Activity

Rename the following things after people you know. You could call a bicycle a **billcycle** after someone named Bill. An airplane could be renamed an **airsmith** for someone whose last name is Smith.

pencil _____   toaster _____

hamburger _____   refrigerator _____

television _____   piano _____

46

saxophone: a musical instrument found in many school bands and named for Adolphe Sax, the German who invented it.

silhouette: when the outline of a face is filled in with black, it is called a silhouette. Named for Etienne de Silhouette, a French politician.

sideburns: hair grown on the sides of a man's face by the ears. Named for Ambrose Burnside, a Union leader in the American Civil War. Sideburns were first called burnsides.

stroganoff: beef stroganoff is a food named for Count Paul Stroganoff, a Russian diplomat.

teddy bear: a stuffed toy bear named for Theodore Roosevelt, an American President. The toy was named for him because he once refused to kill a bear while on a hunting trip.

zeppelin: unlike a blimp a zeppelin is an airship with a rigid shell. It was used during World War I and named for Count Ferdinand Von Zeppelin, a German scientist.

Activity

Use your dictionary to find out the names of the people that the following words came from. Write the names next to the words below.

America _____

Celsius _____

galvanized _____

bowie knife _____

chauvanist _____

gerrymander _____

The Story of Reverend Spooner

Reverend William Spooner was an educator and clergyman in England. He became famous for his creative and humorous mistakes while teaching at a college. Instead of saying the words "conquering kings," he once said "kinquering congs." He is famous for the time he introduced a hymn to his students as "kinquering congs their tatles tike." The words "tatles tike" should be "titles take." Reverend Spooner used these mistakes to make his sermons and lectures more interesting, and his students loved them. The Reverend was once upset at a student for wasting two terms in school. He said, "You have deliberately tasted two worms...."

His students began inventing their own creative and humorous mistakes, and they called them **spoonerisms.** Two famous spoonerisms are "let me sew you to your sheet" and "you are occupewing my pie." The real sentences that they come from are "let me show you to your seat" and "you are occupying my pew."

Activity: Invent three of your own **spoonerisms.** First write a real sentence. It can be about anything. Next, mix up some of the letters in some of the words until the sentence comes out sounding funny. Follow the example below.

Real Sentence   I think I failed my spelling test.

Spoonerism   I fink i thailed my telling spest.

Real Sentence _____

Spoonerism _____

Real Sentence _____

Spoonerism _____

Real Sentence _____

Spoonerism _____

Naming the Automobile

In the middle of the last century, work was being done in several countries to invent the **automobile.** During this time the automobile had no name, and inventors had the opportunity to make up new words to describe it. It took many years for the word **automobile** to become part of our language. The word itself combines two Latin words: **auto** means ''self'' and **mobile** means ''moving.'' The two words together mean ''self-moving.''

Following are a few of the many names that were suggested to describe the automobile. Most of them will sound funny and strange to you **because** you probably never heard them before. At one time the word **automobile** also sounded strange to people.

autogen	electromobile
autogo	ipsometer
autokinet	molectros
autopher	self-motor
autovic	trundle

Activity

The word **bicycle** combines two Latin words: **bi** comes from a word meaning ''two,'' and **cycle** comes from a word meaning ''circle.'' A bicycle really is a ''two-circle'' machine. Invent four of your own words to describe a **bicycle.** You may wish to invent some funny words. For example, **wheeleo, footmobile,** or **crankercycle.**

_____

_____

Food for Thought

When words are used **figuratively**, their meanings change. The expression **food for thought** really means "something to think about." Write the real meanings of these figures of speech that have to do with food.

1. The kid liked to "ham it up." _____

2. The car was a real "lemon." _____

3. Mom and Dad "bring home the bacon." _____

4. The test was a "piece of cake." _____

5. Don't be a "hot dog" on the team. _____

6. Knowledge is the "spice of life." _____

7. You have "good taste" in clothes. _____

8. We had a "sour" experience. _____

9. They were all "sandwiched" together. _____

10. It was a "tasteless" joke. _____

11. That was a very "sweet" thought. _____

12. "Chew on that" for awhile. _____

13. They "chewed the fat" all day. _____

14. The music was "bland." _____

15. Don't "butter me up." _____

Naming Our Foods

Chicken fat, called **schmaltz** in Yiddish, is used in traditional Jewish cooking. When a food name is used figuratively, its meaning changes. When something is sentimental, it is said to be "schmaltzy."

apricot: from an Arabic word meaning "ripens before its time."
bread: from an Old English word meaning "fragment."
broccoli: from an Italian word meaning "little spike."
cabbage: from a Latin word meaning "head."
cauliflower: from French meaning "flower of the cabbage."
chocolate: from a Nahuatl word meaning "bitter water."
corn: from an Old English word meaning "worn down particle."
date: from a Latin word meaning "finger."
lettuce: from a Latin word meaning "milk-giving plant."
mushroom: from a French word meaning "moss."
omelette: from a French word meaning "thin blade of a sword."
onion: from a Latin word meaning "unity."
pumpkin: from a Greek word meaning "ripen in the sun."
radish: from a Latin word meaning "root."
spaghetti: from an Italian word meaning "string."
tapioca: from Portugese meaning "squeeze out the dregs."
vegetable: from a Latin word meaning "to enliven."

Activity

Here is a phoney word origin: "**chocolate:** from the language of Munchkin where ancient children wrote with chocolate and were happy to 'eat their words.' " Invent two of your own phoney word origins for the names of popular foods.

Food _____ Origin _____

_____

Food _____ Origin _____

_____

Incredible Edible Words

Food names have come into English from many languages. Dutch has given us **cole slaw, cookie,** and **waffle.** French has given us **gravy, jelly,** and **pastry.** American Indian languages have given us **chili, chocolate, hickory, maize, pecan, potato, succotash, squash,** and **tomato.** Italian has contributed **macaroni, ravioli, pizza, salami,** and **spaghetti. Yogurt** is from Turkish, and **bagel** is from Yiddish. **Orange** and **syrup** are from Arabic. German has given us **noodle, pretzel,** and **sauerkraut.** African languages have given us **banana, gumbo, okra,** and **yam.** Spanish has given us **avocado, cocoa, taco,** and **tortilla.** Chinese has contributed **chow mein, chop suey,** and **tea.** The spellings of food names are usually changed when they enter English to make them easier to read. The American Indian word **squontersquashes** was shortened to **squash.** Here are food names with their original spellings. What foods are they in modern English? The sound of each word will give you a clue.

alemette (French) _____

batata (Tiano) _____

caseus (Latin) _____

chou-fleur (French) _____

isfanakh (Arabic) _____

ke-tsiap (Chinese) _____

khanda (Sanskrit) _____

koekje (Dutch) _____

koolsa (Dutch) _____

limun (Persian) _____

mete (Old English) _____

narang (Persian) _____

nyami (African) _____

rotabagge (Swedish) _____

sharbah (Persian) _____

t'e (Chinese) _____

YOU'LL NEVER CATCH UP TO ME!

Words that People Own

If you decide to manufacture a soft drink don't call it **Coca-Cola.** You can call it **Jazzy-Cola,** but not **Coca-Cola.** The names **Coca-Cola** and **Coke** are registered brand names, or trademarks, of a company. **Brand names** are special names given to products by the companies that make them. **Thermos** is a brand name, or trademark, of the company that makes these special vacuum containers. Other companies may make similar containers, but they are not allowed to call them thermoses. **Vaseline** is a brand name for petroleum jelly, and **Q-Tips** is a brand name for cotton swabs. Here are other popular brand names: **Kleenex, Jell-O, Tylenol, Osterizer, Celluloid, Frigidaire, Dictaphone, Pyrex, Teflon, Coleman Stove,** and **Saran Wrap.** Many of us think of the brand names as the names of the products themselves. It would be like thinking that light bulbs are called "general electrics," or that washing machines are called "maytags." We all know that there are many kinds of light bulbs and washing machines. When you **Simonize** a car you are using a particular brand of car wax. When you buy a pair of **Levi's,** you are buying one brand of jeans.

Companies invest a lot of money in their products. They are very protective of their brand names in the same way that you are protective of your property. The company that makes **Sanka** coffee is very careful to let us know that their name is a brand name. The same is true with the company that makes **Formica,** which is a laminated plastic used on counter tops. At one time the word **cola** was owned by the **Coca-Cola** company. In the Supreme Court it was decided that the word **cola** was so popular that other businesses had the right to use it. The words **Band-Aid** and **Xerox** have become so popular that the companies who make them have actually had to go to court to keep their brand names. In the past many companies have lost the right to use their own brand names exclusively. The following words were once brand names, but can now be used by anyone: **cellophane, mimeograph, aspirin, aerosol, linoleum, shredded wheat, nylon, kerosene,** and **zipper.**

Activity

Invent a slogan and a brand name for your own imaginative cola drink. For example, "Add some fizz to your divided life with **Math-Cola.''**

A Zoo of Words

The word **animal** comes from the Latin word **anima** meaning "breath of life." Animals are **animate** beings, and **animators** give the "breath of life" to pictures.

caterpillar: from the Latin words **catta** + **pilosus.** Together they add up to an imaginative name for a caterpillar, "hairy-cat."

chameleon: from the Greek word **khamaileon** meaning "dwarf-lion."

crocodile: from the Greek word **krokodeilos** meaning "gravel-worm."

deer: until the 13th century all wild animals were deers. Today the meaning of the word has narrowed to a particular animal.

dinosaur: from the Latin word **deinos-sauros** meaning "fearful lizard."

duck: from the Old English word **duce** meaning "diver."

flamingo: clip off the last letter and you have its description, "flaming." From the Latin word **flamma** meaning "flame."

hippopotamus: from the Greek **hippos-potamos** meaning "river-horse."

leopard: from the Greek **leopardos** meaning "lion-tiger."

moose: from the Algonquian word **moosu** meaning "stripper of bark."

Activity

Rename each of the following animals with two words that describe their actions. For example you might call a **beaver** the "tail-hammer."

snake _____   horse _____

kitten _____   monkey _____

shark _____   snake _____

YOU BIG WORM!

A Zoo of Words

Early American settlers used simple, sometimes poetic, words to name the animals they saw: **blue jay, bullfrog,** and **catfish.** Bird names often come from their sounds: **chickadee, hummingbird,** and **whippoorwill.**

octopus: from the Greek words **octo + pous** meaning "eight-foot."

opossum: from the Algonquian word **appossoum** meaning "white-beast."

orangutan: from the Malay word **oranghutan** meaning "forest-man."

oriole: from the Latin word **aureolus** meaning "golden."

poodle   from the German word **pudelhund** meaning "splash-dog." The word poodle has the same origin as the word **puddle.**

porcupine: from the French **porc d' espine** meaning "spine-porker."

raccoon: from the Algonquian word **raugraoughcun** meaning "scratcher."

spider: from the Old English word **spithra** meaning "spinner."

Activity

The word **pelican** comes from the Greek word **pelekys** meaning "ax." Don't get confused, but what the Greeks called a **pelican** we call a **woodpecker.** Why is the word "ax" a good name for a woodpecker?

_____

_____

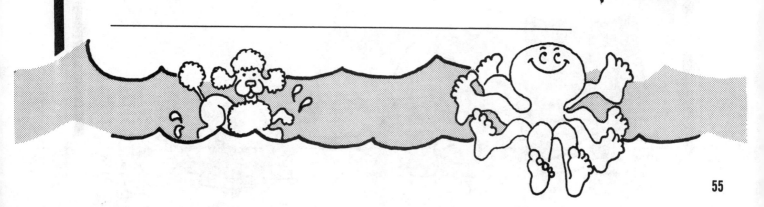

55

A Flock of Animal Names

1. Many young animals and birds are called **bables** or **younglings.** Some young animals and birds have their own special names. A **cheeper** is a baby quail. A **cockerel** is a baby rooster. An **elver** is a baby eel. Use a dictionary to find out which animal or bird each of the following younglings is named for. Some younglings' names are used to name several animals. For example, a **pup** is a baby dog, sea lion, seal, fox, or wolf. Write just one answer in each space.

cub _____ cygnet _____ fawn _____

fledgling _____ joey _____ kit _____

owlet _____ tadpole _____ yearling _____

2. Our language has many special words that name groups of animals. Gorillas live in **bands,** and lions live in **prides.** A group of geese is called a **gaggle,** and some fish travel in **schools.** Some group names are very unusual. There is an **exaltation** of larks, and a **clowder** of cats. There is a **husk** of hares, and a **skulk** of foxes. Use a dictionary to find out which animals the following groups name.

A clutch of _____ A colony of _____ A drove of _____

A flock of _____ A pack of _____ A swarm of _____

3. Animals sometimes have special names depending on whether they are males or females. People are called **men** and **women, boys** and **girls.** Use a dictionary to help you fill in the blank spaces on the lines below.

A male horse is a _____ . A female horse is a _____ .

A baby male horse is a _____ . A baby female horse is a _____ .

A ewe is a female _____ . A ram is a male _____ .

A cow is a female _____ . A bull is a male _____ .

Foxy Words

We have given "poetic" meanings to words that name animals. Extending the meanings of words keeps our language healthy. Sometimes we use the names of animals **figuratively.** Teams are named for them: **Rams, Falcons, Cubs,** and **Dolphins.** Clubs are named for them: **Elks** and **Lions.** Even tools and machines are named for them: **monkey wrench** and **bulldozer.** American Indian clans are often named for animals: **Bear** Clan and **Turtle** Clan. There are the **Snake** River and the **Salmon** River, and cities named **Buffalo** and **Alligator.** In politics there are **hawks** and **doves.** Stock investors speak about **bull** and **bear** markets, and everyone likes to eat **hot dogs.** What do the animal names mean in the following lines?

We **monkey** around. _____

Don't **bully** me. _____

I feel **batty**. _____

He felt **sheepish**. _____

Something's **fishy**. _____

They **lionized** her. _____

We **hogged** the food. _____

The test was a **bear**. _____

I'm **ape** over words. _____

It **bugs** me. _____

You sure are **foxy**. _____

Sometimes I feel **mousey**. _____

Clipped Words

Many words are made shorter by **clipping** off letters or syllables. Some words come into English from another language as long words and are **clipped** to make them easier to speak and write. The word **squash** has been **clipped** from the long Algonquin Indian word **askutasquash.**

ad from **advertisement**	**ammo** from **ammunition**
amp from **ampere**	**bus** from **omnibus**
cab from **cabriolet**	**cello** from **violoncello**
cheat from **escheat**	**fan** from **fanatic**
flu from **influenza**	**gypsy** from **Egyptian**
hack from **hackney**	**hood** from **hoodlum**
lone from **alone**	**mend** from **amend**
prop from **property**	**rhino** from **rhinoceros**
sample from **example**	**spend** from **dispend**
sport from **disport**	**still** from **distillery**
vibes from **vibrations**	**wig** from **periwig**

Activity: Write the words from which these shortened words are taken.

bike _____   burger _____   exam _____

fridge _____   gas _____   gym _____

math _____   phone _____   photo _____

plane _____   sax _____   vet _____

OMNIBUS

CLIPPED WORDS

A word phase can be clipped down to a single word. The single word keeps the same meaning as the phrase. The words "capital letters" can be **clipped** down to the word "capitals." The word "capitals" can then be **clipped** further into the shorter word "caps."

chum comes from **chamber fellow**
bye from **good-bye** from **God be with you**
grid comes from **gridiron**
Halloween comes from **All-Hallows-Evening**
hi-fi comes from **high fidelity**
hobby comes from **hobbyhorse**
mob comes from **mobile vulgus**
mutt comes from **muttonhead**
nincompoop comes from **non-compos-mentis**
patter comes from **patter-noster**
piano comes from **piano-e-forte**
preemie comes from **premature baby**
pub comes from **public house**
snap comes from **snapshot**
zoo comes from **zoological gardens**

Activity
Invent your own clipped words from the following phrases. For example, the phrase "absolutely excellent" could be **clipped** and **blended** into the new word **abex.** "I feel **abex** today!"

behavior problem _____   doing homework _____

incredibly fantastic _____   munching junk food _____

taking megavitamins _____   walking the dog _____

Sometimes new words are coined by connecting two entire words, and they are called **joined** words. The word **skyscraper** joins the words **sky** and **scrape**. Some joined words use the names of our body parts. The word **footpath** combines the words **foot** and **path**. Some words like **merry-go-round** and **play-by-play** even join three whole words.

Joined Words Naming Different Things

airplane, basketball, blackboard, doghouse, grasshopper, hardware, keepsake, landlord, lawnmower, make-believe, nighttime, pancake, playground, quicksand, rawhide, sandbox, teaspoon, whatever

Joined Words Naming Body Parts

armchair, armhole, earache, earmuff, earphone, earring, eyebrow, eyeglasses, eyelid, eyewitness, fingernail, fingerpaint, football, hairbrush, handball, handshake, headrest, headstrong, jawbone, skindiver, toenail, toothache, toothbrush

Activity

Invent your own **joined** words to describe a new kind of food, animal, machine, and sport. For example, combine the word **eagle** with **beagle** and you get an **eaglebeagle.** Remember, you can't shorten either of the words. You have to use both complete words.

food _____ animal _____

machine _____ sport _____

Portmanteau Words

Lewis Carroll, author of **Alice in Wonderland,** liked inventing new words. One way he did this was to **blend** existing words together. He called these **portmanteau words,** named for a special kind of suitcase that has two compartments. He said that two words blended together is like a **portmanteau** because you get "two meanings packed in one word." He blended **snort** with **chuckle** and came up with **chortle.** These kinds of words are also known as **blend words,** and they contribute many useful words to our language. The word **smog** blends **smoke** and **fog.** The word **medicare** blends **medical** and **care.**

1. What **blend words** comes from the following word pairs?

glare + shimmer = _____   **motor + hotel =** _____

smack + bash = _____   **flame + glare =** _____

not + ever = _____   **twist + swirl =** _____

2. What **two** words do the following **word blends** come from?

bookmobile =   _____ + _____

brunch =   _____ + _____

newscast =   _____ + _____

motorcade =   _____ + _____

dictaphone =   _____ + _____

bloodmobile =   _____ + _____

3. Invent your own humorous **portmanteau** words. Blend **breakfast** with **supper** and make **supfast.** Blend **sleep** with **pillow** and make **slillow.**

_____ + _____ = _____

_____ + _____ = _____

_____ + _____ = _____

Acronyms

An acronym is a special kind of shortened word or name made by connecting the first letter or letters of several words **NASA** is an agency whose letters stand for National Aeronautics and Space Administration. **Nabisco** is a company whose letters stand for National Biscuit Company.

CARE: an organization that helps people in many countries. The letters stand for "Cooperative for American Relief Everywhere."

Jeep: A vehicle first made for the Army and called a **G.P.** which stands for "general purpose" vehicle. The name **jeep** was invented later and comes from the sound of the letters **G.P.**

radar: a safety device used to detect the presence of objects that cannot be seen. The letters stand for "radio detecting and ranging."

scuba: people can breathe underwater with **scuba** gear. The letters stand for "self-contained underwater breathing apparatus."

sonar: a device used by ships to detect objects with beams of sound. The letters stand for "sound navigation and ranging."

Zip Code: a number code that aids postal workers in sorting mail. The letters stand for "zoning improvement plan."

Activity

Create your own humorous **acronym.** Rename some imaginary club in your school. For example, **GABBERS** which stands for "girls and boys beyond emotion, reason, and sanity."

acronym _____

definition _____

Initialisms

An **initialism** is a series of letters that stand for names or words. Do you live in the U.S.A.? The letters stand for "United States of America." An **initialism** is a special kind of code used to shorten words and names. The letters F.D.R. stand for an American President whose name was Franklin Delano Roosevelt.

Activities

1. What words and names do the following **initialisms** stand for? Use a dictionary with a special section for abbreviations.

   BLT sandwich _____   CB radio _____

   J.F.K. _____   O.K. _____

   S.O.S. _____   TV _____

2. What **initialisms** are used to stand for the following names and words?

   absent without leave _____

   cash on delivery _____

   extra sensory perception _____

   intelligence quotient _____

   patrol torpedo boat _____

   United Nations _____

Fact

The agency called the **E.I.D.E.B.O.E.W.A.B.E.W.** for short was better known as "Economic Intelligence Division of the Enemy Branch of the Office of Economic Warfare Analysis of the Board of Economic Warfare."

The Sounds We Make

The sounds we use to express emotions are heard and written differently in other languages. Santa Claus is famous for his jolly **ho-ho-ho.** In the Russian language **ho-ho-ho** is written as **kho-khot,** and in a language called Sanskrit it is **ka-khat.** Santa Claus always keeps an international dictionary with him. In English we describe the sound of a kiss as a **smack.** In Spanish a kiss sound is **mua.** Following are a few people-sounds as they are heard and written in different languages.

BLAH: a sound of disgust
fi, pfutt, zut (French), pfui (German), uffa (Italian), pro (Latin), huyoruf (Spanish), phooey (Yiddish).

HEY: a call to get someone's attention
eia (Ancient Greek), ao (Italian), eho (Latin).

OUCH: a sound of pain
boi (Finnish), aie (French), jaj (Hungarian), aio (Italian), itai (Japanese), ay (Spanish).

WOE: a sound of sorrow
vai (Armenian), wai (Ancient Gothic), pheu (Ancient Greek), vae (Latin), avoi (Ancient Persian), gwae (Welsh), oi-vay (Yiddish).

Activity
Imagine if things that are not alive had emotions. What words would the things listed below use to express their feelings. Use your imagination to create original sounds for each thing.

A volcano expressing anger: _____

A cloud expressing pain: _____

A rock expressing disgust: _____

What Sound Did You Hear?

How do you describe the sound of a heartbeat? Thump-thump? Ba-boom? Patter-patter? Each of us hears sounds a little differently. There are no words that are exactly right to describe a particular sound. In a language called Sanskrit, the sound of a heart is **ki-kira,** the **whiz** of an arrow is **chish-cha,** and a **splash** of water is **p-hat.** The English word **gurgle** is **glut-glut** in Latin and **glu-glu** in Italian. Following are a few sound words as they are heard and described in different languages. Do they sound funny to you? Think of how English sound-words must sound to people who speak other languages.

CRASH: the sound of something falling
hua-la-la (Chinese), kling (Danish), krats (Finnish), chir-churr (Hungarian).

DING-A-LING: the sound of a bell
kili (Finnish), dringh (Greek), drin (Italian), tlim (Portuguese).

WHAM: something being hit
pan (French), patapunf (Italian), catrapuz-bum (Portuguese), cataplum (Spanish).

SNIP-SNIP: scissors cutting
su-su (Chinese), krits-krits (Greek), cri-cri (Italian), terre-terre (Portuguese), riqui-riqui (Spanish).

Activity

The word **clap** describes the sound of many things. Clap your hands slowly while holding them close to your ears. Spell the sound with the letters you think you hear. For example, "bllaatt." Then spell the other kinds of clapping sounds that are listed below.

two hands clapping: _____

a group clapping hands: _____

a book closing: _____

Words from Sounds

There are many words in our language that come from sounds. There are sounds from animals, sounds from nature, and sounds from machines. Below is a list of sound-words. Where does each of the sounds come from? Write your answers in the blank spaces. You will find that some sounds come from several sources. The sound of a **pop** can come from a balloon bursting, a cork coming out of a bottle, or from popcorn being made.

babble	howl	
bang	jingle	
beep-beep	moo	
boom	murmur	
bow-wow	nay	
buzz	ping	
chirp	plop	
clang	pop	
clap	purr	
ding-a-ling	roar	
fizz	sizzle	
flutter	snort	
growl	swish	
gurgle	toot-toot	
hiss	zip	

The Cat's Meow

English speaking cats like to say **meow,** but Japanese speaking cats prefer to say **nyah.** In Russia the cats say **mjau,** and the French cats prefer to say **miaou.** Spanish speaking cats say **miau,** Israeli cats say **yim-yum,** and Arabic cats prefer a **nau-nau.** Actually, cats all around the world speak the same language. Different people just hear **meow** in different ways. Is a **meow** better than a **nyah**? Not really. Listen very closely to a cat's meow sometime. You just might hear your own cat speaking Japanese.

In English we have several words to describe the barking of a dog: **woof-woof, ruff-ruff,** and **bow-wow.** Japanese dogs prefer to say **wan-wan,** and Russian dogs prefer to say **gav-gav** or **vas-vas.** Dogs in Iceland, on the other hand, simply say **voff.** Now, Rumanian dogs say **ham-ham,** and Turkish dogs are fond of saying **gau-gau.** Arabic dogs utter a **chau-chau,** and Irish dogs whisper a polite **amh-amh.** Which sound is the right one? Ask a duck.

Every educated American duck will tell you **quack-quack.** But the French ducks argue every **quack-quack** with a **coin-coin.** The Finnish ducks exclaim **kvaak-kvaak,** and the Russian ducks respond with a **kva-kva.** The Danish ducks suggest **rap-rap,** until the Mexican ducks proclaim **cua-cua.** At this point the Japanese duck gently suggests **ga-ga,** and the Chinese ducks answer with a **ya-ya.**

You hear a bird say **tweet,** but in Israel they hear **tzip,** and in Thailand they hear **jip.** You hear a cow say **moo,** but in France they hear **meuh.** You may wake up to a **coq-a-doodle-doo,** but in Israel they wake up to a **coo-coo-re-co.** The same rooster proclaims a **kuckeliku** in Sweden, a **quiquiriqui** in Spain, a **kokek-koko** in Japan, a **kikiriki** in Germany, a **cucuirgu** in Rumania. A **ribbit** to you is a **kero-kero** in Japan. A **gobble-gobble** to you is a **ko-ko-ko** in China, a **cotcodac** in Rumania, a **kuku** in Japan, and a **cot-cot** in France. Your favorite **oink** is a Russian's favorite **khru-khru** and a Rumanian's favorite **guits-guits.** A **hee-haw** to your donkey is a **hi-han** to a French donkey, and **i-o** to an Italian or Chinese donkey, and an **i-a** to a German or Russian donkey.

Activity

Invent new words to describe the sounds of the following animals. There are no right or wrong answers.

horse _____ sheep _____ fish _____

bee _____ lion _____ worm _____

67

Euphemisms

A **euphemism** is a word or phrase used to make another word sound better. Some **euphemisms** are used to hide the real meanings of words with emotional or negative meanings. For example, a **battle** can be called a **strategic engagement** so it won't sound as bad. Some **euphemisms** are useful, and some make our language vague and complicated. When they hide the real meanings of words they make what is known as **gobbledegook, whitewashed words,** or **double-talk.** Many words used in formal school and government reports contain **euphemisms.** A student's grade might be called a **performance standing,** or a **test** might be called a **skills evaluation.** Draw lines to connect the words on the left and the **euphemisms** that replace them on the right.

garbage man	pressure garment assembly
secretary	intellectually disadvantaged
spacesuit	sanitation worker
truant officer	administrative aid
died	building supervisor
spy	animal welfare officer
stupid	attendance teacher
custodian	intelligence agent
dog catcher	passed away

Activity

Write a humorous paragraph about your school using euphemisms from the list above.

_____

_____

_____

_____

From Euphemisms to Gobbledegook

A **euphemism** is a word or phrase that tries to make something sound better. Years ago the word **cemetery** was used to replace the word **graveyard**. Today **memorial park** is sometimes used instead of cemetery because people think it sounds better. The word **jail** was upgraded with the word **prison,** and **prison** is slowly being replaced by the term **correctional facility.** The guards are **correctional officers,** the **warden** is a **superintendent,** and the **prisoners** are **residents.** Some euphemisms are used to show respect. The term **senior citizen** is much nicer than the term **old person.** The word **inexpensive** is often used instead of the word **cheap** even though they mean the same thing. Euphemisms can be used to sway our opinions. Sometimes the word **war** is called a **police action** because it sounds less dangerous. Even though a bomb is called a **strategic deterrent,** it can still explode. The **tax collectors** may now be **revenue agents,** but they still collect our money.

Gobbledegook is defined as wordy and unclear language. This can happen when we use too many complex words to describe something simple. When a euphemism goes too far, it can become **gobbledegook.** Imagine calling a **pen** a "manual ink processor," or a **playground** an "out-of-doors kiddy recreational fun and fitness surface." A congressman once discovered some funny examples of gobbledegook used by the government. A **shovel** was called a "combat emplacement evacuator." **Oil drums** used around road obstructions were called "impact attenuation devices." Someone even called a **lie** a "terminological inexactitude." That's gobbledegook!

Activity

Invent some gobbledegook phrases for the following words. For example, **school** could be called a "temporary learning detainment center."

hate _____

homework _____

lie _____

school _____

The Meanings of Words Can Change

1. The word **sturdy** used to mean "harsh." Its meaning has been **rais-ed** to mean "strong." The meaning of a **raised** word gets better.

annoy meant "seriously hurt"
careful meant "nervous"
clown meant "clumsy"
fond meant "foolish"
marshal meant "horseshoer"
pretty meant "sly"
priceless meant "no value"

brave meant "mean"
constable meant "stable attendant"
court meant "a place for chickens"
jaunt meant "a tiring trip"
nice meant "foolish"
prestige meant "trick"
respect meant "spy"

2. The word **cunning** used to mean "skill." Its meaning has been **lowered** to mean "sly" or "sneaky." The meaning of a **lowered** word gets worse.

artificial meant "true to art"
idiot meant "private person"
puny meant "younger"
sinister meant "left-handed"
smirk meant "smile"
stink meant "any smell"
tinker meant "maker of pots"

bribe meant "piece of bread"
plastic meant "flexible"
silly meant "blessed"
sly meant "wise"
snob meant "shoemaker's helper"
stupid meant "amazed"
villain meant "farm worker"

Activity

Write the **old** meanings of the underlined words next to each sentence.

My **puny** brother is **sinister**. _____ _____

Robbers are **brave** and **pretty**. _____ _____

They are **plastic** and **sly**. _____ _____

He is **careful** in **court**. _____ _____

HERE, HAVE A SHOVEL!

The Meanings of Words Can Change

1. The word **companion** used to mean "someone who eats with you." Its meaning has been **widened** to mean "someone who does anything with you."

    banquet meant "light dessert"
    bread meant "fragment"
    cash meant "box"
    humor meant "fluid"
    rocket meant "fireworks"
    squirrel meant "tail"

    barn meant "place for barley"
    cafeteria meant "coffee pot"
    comrade meant "roommate"
    manufacture meant "made by hand"
    salary meant "money for salt"
    town meant "fence"

2. The word **comedy** used to mean "a play with a happy ending." Its meaning has been **narrowed** to mean "a play that is funny."

    bible meant "book"
    engine meant "active person"
    liquor meant "fluid"
    meat meant "food"
    pipe meant "musical instrument"
    starve meant "to die"

    deer meant "wild animal"
    girl meant "boy or girl"
    lumber meant "room for wood"
    niece meant "boy or girl"
    soon meant "now"
    stove meant "heated room"

Activity

Write a humorous dialogue between two people who misunderstand each other. One uses words with their modern meanings, and the other uses words with their old meanings.

_____

_____

_____

_____

_____

The Name of the Game

Badminton: a game played on a court with rackets. Inverted in India, and named for the estate of the Duke of Beaufort in England.

Baseball: played since the time of the American Revolution. It actually started as a game called **prisoner's base** in the fifteenth century. Named for the four bases that must be touched in order to score.

Basketball: a game invented in Massachusetts in 1891 with players attempting to throw a large ball into peach baskets nailed to a wall. Some early games were played with as many as fifty players on each team.

Bowling: played in Egypt over 5,000 years ago. Only a few hundred years ago it was forbidden by several English kings. King Richard II said the game was too easy, and it gave no training for fighting.

Cards: different kinds of card games were played as early as the tenth century in China and in the twelfth century in England.

Chess: the name comes from the Old French word **esches.** It was developed in Persia and called **shah-mat** which means "the King is dead." The sound of the word became the chess term checkmate.

Activity

Some sports are played on **fields** (baseball, football), others are played on **courts** (basketball, tennis). Games are usually played on **boards.** Invent, name, and describe your own sport or game.

name of the game _____

description _____

_____

_____

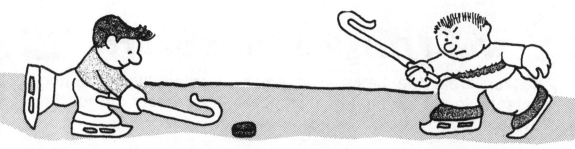

The Name of the Game

Dice: many popular games are played with dice. The name comes from the Latin word **datum** which means "given." When you roll dice you are "given" a chance. Dice have been used in games for 10,000 years.

Golf: developed in Scotland in the twelfth century. It is possible that the name comes from a Dutch word **kolf** which means "club."

Hockey: named for an Old French word **hoquet** meaning "shepherd's staff." It was played in Persia thousands of years ago by the Ancient Greeks and by the native Americans.

Marathon: a twenty-six-mile footrace named for the city of Marathon in Greece. A runner named Pheidippides ran from Marathon to Athens to announce that the Greeks had defeated the Persians in war. It is said that he dropped dead after announcing the good news.

Soccer: known as **football** in Europe. The name **soccer** comes from the word **association.**

Tennis: no one is certain where the name comes from, but it was played in France and England hundreds of years ago. The name may come from the Middle English word **tenetz** meaning "receive" or "take." The name could come from the Old French word **tenie** which was the string over which the tennis ball was hit.

Activity

How did **Ping-Pong** get its name? Take a guess and write your answer below. Look up the word in a dictionary and find out how the game really got its name. How close was your guess?

_____

_____

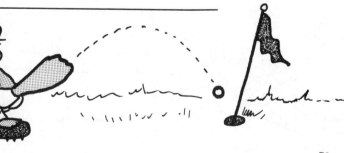

Word Origins from Sports

Amateur: from the Latin word **amor** meaning "love." Since amateurs do not get money to compete, they must do it for the "love" of their sport.

Arena: from the Latin word **harena** meaning "sand." Sand was used by the Romans to soak up the blood from victims thrown to the lions.

Athlete: from the Greek word **athlon** meaning "prize." Today an athlete is a person who participates in a sport, not the prize.

Ball: from the Greek word **ballein** meaning "to throw." Today the ball is the object that is thrown.

Game: from the Old English word **ghem** meaning "to leap joyfully," and from **gamen** meaning "fun." Games are fun.

Race: from the Old English word **raes** meaning "swift course," and from the Sanskrit word **rish** meaning "to flow." A race is kind of a "flow."

Racket: from the Arabic word **rahat** meaning "palm of the hand," which a racket looks like.

Score: from the Old Norse word **skor** meaning "notch." Scores were kept by making notches in wood.

Umpire: from the Latin word **noumpere** meaning "not equal." Since umpires are like judges they are not equal to the players.

Activity
The word **sport** comes from the Latin word **desporato** meaning "to carry away." What is your opinion about the connection between this word and its original meaning? Write your opinion below.

_____

_____

Body Parts with New Meanings

We have given new "poetic" meanings to words that name parts of our bodies. This is one way our language keeps growing. Sometimes we name a part of the body in a phrase which gives the word a metaphorical meaning. In poetry a **metaphor** changes one thing into something else. The word **heart** means **center** or **middle** in the phrase "the heart of the problem." Using body parts with new meanings helps us to understand things better. What do the body parts mean in the following common phrases? Write your answers in the blank spaces.

arm of the chair _____

backbone of the book _____

breath of spring _____

elbow of a pipe _____

eye of a hurricane _____

foot of a hill _____

hands of a clock _____

head of a pin _____

legs of a table _____

neck of a bottle _____

shoulder of a road _____

tongue of a shoe _____

wing of a building _____

Some Long-Long-Long-Long Words

Many long words are shortened when they enter English from other languages. The word "fan" is from the Latin word **fanaticus.** The word **raccoon** and **squash** come from the American Indian words **raugraoughcun,** and **isquontersquashe.** Ancient Greek did not have spaces between words, and every sentence looked like one long word. **Canyoureadthissentencewithoutthespaces**? Many languages use **compound** words. Several words are connected together and are read as one long word. The Hawaiian language has a compound word for the "triggerfish." They call it a **humunukunukuapuaa.** The German language also has some incredible compound words. There is a law to help war prisoners known as **Kriegsgefangenanentschadigungsgesetz.** Someone once tried to translate the Bible into Algonguian and came up with the word **nummatchekodtantamoonganunnonoas** for the English phrase "our loves."

The Walt Disney movie *Mary Poppins* gave us the long nonsense word **supercalifragilisticexpialidocious.** Scientists have formula words that can have hundreds of letters and numbers. The formula word for the chemical **cortisone** is **17,21-dihydrooxypregn-4-ene,3,11,21-trione.** Astronomers use a device which is called a **spectroheliokinematograph** which measures sunlight with a motion picture camera. Looking at the meaning of its **roots** helps us understand the word. **Spectro** from Latin means "to look at." **Helio** from Greek means "sun." **Kinema** from Greek means "to move." **Graph** from Greek means "to write." Put the root parts together and we get "to look at-sun-to move-to write." One of the longest words in the English language names a lung disease caused by invisible volcanic dust. The dashes between the **root** parts will help you to read it: **pneumono-ultra-micro-scopic-silico-volcano-koni-osis.** Put the meaning of the root parts together and we get "lung-beyond-small-to see-quartz-volcano-dust-condition." Imagine that on a spelling test!

Activity

On the first line create your own long-long-long-long nonsense word. On the second line write its meaning. Use some real Latin and Greek roots.

_____

_____

Student Activity Answer Key

Page 3: brightness; foot; heart; heaven; light; moon; night; star; sun.

Page 5: ax; center; check; civilize; color; connection; cider; flavor; gray; honor; jewelry; labor; odor; neighbor; offense; program; pajamas; story; traveler; wagon.

Page 8: wan-trust = suspicion; wan-wit = folly; wan-thrift = extravagance; wan-grace = wicked; wan-hope = despair.

Page 22: school **spirit** = positive attitude; **spirited** debate = lively; supernatural **spirit** = ghost or being; **spirit** of fun = mood.

Page 23: anchor; ark; box; chalk; circle; comet; dish; dragon; fact; fever; hospital; miracle; nature; public; quiet; write.

Page 28: Tree + Tree = Forest; Fire + Cart = Railroad; Sun + Horizon = Dawn; Brain + Heart = Think; Stream + Mouth = Words; Woman + Child = Good.

Page 31: telegraph, telemeter, telephone, telephoto lens, telethermoscope, television, televisor.

Page 34: Atlantic Ocean; Olympic Games.

Page 41: Artois, France; Cologne, Germany; India; Spain; Tobago Island; Turkey.

Page 42: Attica, Greece; Lima, Peru; Madras, India; Mosul, Iraq; Phasis River, Russia; Turkey.

Page 44: Michel Begon; Georg Josef Kamel; Leonhard Fuchs; Alexander Garden; Casper Wistar; Johann Gottfried Zinn.

Page 47: Amerigo Vespucci; Anders Celsius; Luigi Galvani; James Bowie; Nicholas Chauvin; Elbridge Gerry.

Page 50: 1. get excited about things; 2. bad; 3. money; 4. easy; 5. show-off; 6. excitement of life; 7. good opinions; 8. bad; 9. packed; 10. bad; 11. nice; 12. think about that; 13. talked; 14. not interesting; 15. soften me up.

Page 52: omelette; potato; cheese; cauliflower; spinach; ketchup; candy; cookie; cole slaw; lemon; meat; orange; yam; rutabaga; sherbert; tea.

Page 56: 1. cub = bear, lion, fox, shark; cygnet = swan; fawn = deer; fledgling = most birds; joey = kangaroo; kit = fox, beaver, rabbit, cat; owlet = owl; tadpole = frog; yearling = horse, sheep, cattle.
2. A clutch of chicks; A colony of ants; A drove of cattle, sheep; A flock of geese, sheep; A pack of wolves, dogs; A swarm of bees.
3. male horse = stallion; female horse = mare; baby male horse = colt; baby female horse = filly; ewe = sheep; ram = sheep; cow = elephant, cattle; bull = elephant, cattle.

Page 57: monkey = play; bully = bother; sheepish = shy, frightened; fishy = suspicious, wrong; lionized = idolized, adored; hogged = took; bear = difficult; ape = wild, crazy; bugs = bothers, annoys; foxy = pretty, handsome; mousey = small, shy.

Page 61: 1. glimmer; motel; smash; flare; never; twirl. 2. book + automobile; breakfast + lunch; news + broadcast; motor + cavalcade; dictate + phone; blood + automobile.

Page 63: 1. bacon, lettuce, & tomato; citizens' band; John Fitzgerald Kennedy; okay; save our ship; television. 2. A.W.O.L., or awol; C.O.D.; e.s.p.; I.Q.; PT Boat; U.N.

Page 68: garbage man = sanitation worker; secretary = administrative aid; spacesuit = pressure garment assembly; truant officer = attendance teacher; died = passed away; spy = intelligence agent; stupid = intellectually disadvantaged; custodian = building supervisor; dog catcher = animal welfare officer.

Page 73: Ping-Pong was named from the sound of the ball hitting the table, similar to the sound word ding-dong. At one time ping-pong was a trademark.

Page 75: arm = side supports; backbone = spine, back column; breath = feeling; elbow = bend, joint; eye = center, middle; foot = bottom; hands = arms, pointers; head = top; legs = bottom supports; neck = upper part; shoulder = side; tongue = flap; wing = side.

Bibliography

Resource Books

Dohan, Mary Helen **Our Own Words**, Penguin Books.
Flexner, Stuart **I Hear America Talking**, Touchstone.
Funk, Wilfred **Word Origins & Their Romantic Stories**, Grosset & Dunlap.
Funk, Charles **Heavens to Betsy**, Harper & Row.
Hook, J.N. **The History of the English Language**, Ronald.
Hixon & Colodny **Words Ways**, American Book Company.
McKnight, George **English Words and Their Background**, Appleton.
Mencken, H.L. **The American Language**, Alfred A. Knopf.
Pei, Mario **Double-Speak in America**, Hawthorn.
Pei, Mario **The Story of Language**, Mentor.
Shipley, Joseph **Dictionary of Word Origins**, Greenwood Press.

Classroom Books

Alexander, Arthur **The Magic of Words**, Prentice-Hall.
Artman, John **Slanguage**, Good Apple.
Charlip, Beth & Ancona **Handtalk**, Parents Magazine Press.
Cottrell, Leonard **Reading the Past**, Crowell-Collier.
Dugan, William **How Our Alphabet Grew**, Golden Press.
Epstein, Sam & Beryl **The First Book of Words**, Franklin Watts.
Irwin, Keith **The Romance of Writing**, Viking.
Laird, Helene & Charlton **The Tree of Language**, World Publishing.
Lambert, Eloise **Our Language**, Lothrop.
Longman, Harold **What's Behind the Word**, Coward, McCann, & Geoghegan.
Ogg, Oscar **The 26 Letters**, Crowell.
Pei, Mario **All About Language**, Lippincott.
Rogers, Frances **Painted Rock to Printed Page**, Lippincott.
Shipley, Joseph **Word Play**, Hawthorn.
Sorel, Nancy **Word People**, American Heritage Press.
Steckler, Arthur **101 Words & How They Began**, Doubleday.
Wiese, Kurt **You Can Write Chinese**, Viking.
Wolff, Diane **Chinese Writing**, Holt.